MAGNIFICENT TIFFANY SILVER

MAGNIFICENT TIFFANY SILVER

JOHN LORING

HARRY N. ABRAMS, INC., PUBLISHERS

PROJECT MANAGER: Margaret Rennolds Chace

EDITOR: Elisa Urbanelli

COPYEDITOR: Sharon AvRutick

DESIGNER: Carol Ann Robson

Library of Congress Cataloging-in-Publication Data

Loring, John.
  Magnificent Tiffany silver / John Loring.
    p. cm.
  ISBN 0–8109–4273–9
  1. Tiffany and Company—History. 2. Silverware—United
States—History—19th century. 3. Silverware—United
States—History—20th century. I. Title.
  NK7198.T5 L67 2001
  739.2'377471—dc21
                                    2001001267

Published in 2001 by Harry N. Abrams, Incorporated, New York
Printed and bound in Japan
10 9 8 7 6 5 4 3 2 1

Harry N. Abrams, Inc.
100 Fifth Avenue
New York, N.Y. 10011
www.abramsbooks.com

Page 1:
⟠ Detail of the Bryant Vase, 1876. ⟠

Page 2:
⟠ This 10½-inch-tall "Elephant's Foot" loving cup designed by Edward C. Moore was one of many pieces with enamel decoration displayed by Tiffany's at the 1889 Paris Exposition. Both sides of the Indian-style cup have pairs of stylized peacocks with enamel plumage and niello eyes and neck. Contemporary reports commended the cup's design and craftsmanship (see page 69). ⟠

CONTENTS

INTRODUCTION

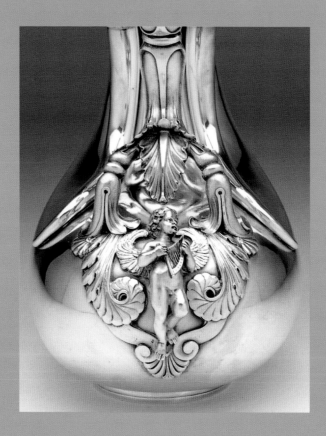

ABOVE:

✐ The Askos Jug (detail), designed by Edward C.
Moore in 1865.

OPPOSITE:

"Four Elements" centerpiece designed and made
by John C. Moore circa 1853 for Tiffany & Co. It is
27½ inches tall, and the gold-lined dish at the top
is 17 inches in diameter. (The silver-plated bronze
base is unmarked and may have been sent to New
York by Tiffany, Reed & Co. in Paris.) The four draped
female figures represent Earth, Air, Fire, and Water,
and the composition is similar to a centerpiece that
Minton's potteries displayed at the Crystal Palace in
London in 1851. Tiffany's displayed this centerpiece
at New York's Crystal Palace Exhibition on Reservoir
Square (now Bryant Park) in 1853–54. It was given to
William Watts Sherman to commemorate his 1851
retirement from the Albany City Bank and was also
included in Tiffany's Loan Exhibition at the 1876
Centennial Exhibition in Philadelphia. In 1874–76
Sherman's son, also named William Watts Sherman,
built a Queen Anne style house in Newport designed
by H. H. Richardson that is considered a masterpiece
of American architecture. The senior Sherman's
centerpiece is now on display at Château-sur-Mer,
one of Newport's historic mansions. ✐

The
Albany City Bank.
to
Watts Sherman,
1851

JOHN C. MOORE

☞ Circa 1850 photograph of John C. Moore (1802–1874). Charles L. Tiffany began to commission silverware from Moore in about 1846, then entered into an exclusive arrangement with Moore's factory when his eldest son, Edward C. Moore, took over its direction in 1851. John C. Moore continued to be active in the firm until 1864. His younger sons, John W. (1837–1912) and Thomas (1843–1919), also worked in the silver factory, John as a silversmith and Thomas as a designer. ☜

From modest beginnings in New York's silver trade in the mid-1840s, Tiffany & Co. had grown to become the world's recognized leader in both silver design and manufacture by the time of the Paris Exposition of 1878. It won the grand prize for silverware at the exposition for its entirely revolutionary introduction of designs liberated from Western Europe's rigid and overused design vocabularies and based on the superbly refined, organic, and naturalistic design aesthetic of Japan. Along with this, the level of craftsmanship in Tiffany's silver shops surpassed that of any competitor, thanks to the immigration to the United States of a workforce of consummate silversmiths who were fleeing the near-continuous political upheavals of mid-nineteenth-century Europe.

Archival photograph of Tiffany's silver factory at 53–55 Prince Street in lower Manhattan, where most of the pieces in this book were produced. This formerly industrial area is now known as SoHo, and the building's lofts are mostly occupied by artists.

Tiffany & Co. made it its business to employ the finest of these immigrant artisans, and it knew how to orchestrate their talents in the production of some of the most exquisitely crafted objects in the history of silver, such as the vast and staggeringly complex, yet harmonious, Saracenic service made for the Mackay family in 1878, which is to this day the greatest single silver tableservice ever produced. These successes were almost solely due to the genius of Tiffany's chief designer and director of its silver shop, Edward C. Moore (1827–1891). Moore was arguably the greatest silversmith of the second half of the nineteenth century, as well as one of its greatest judges of talent; and, although largely unsung, one of the greatest decorative artists America has produced.

In 1837, when Tiffany & Co. (or Tiffany and Young, as it was first named) was founded by Charles Lewis Tiffany, the Moore family had already been established in the silver business in New York for ten years. Edward C. Moore's father, John C. Moore (1802–1874), was the most highly respected New York silversmith and provided fine and stylish silver hollowware to, amongst others, Tiffany's rival, Marquand & Company, and then to its successor, Ball, Tompkins and Black. About 1846, Charles Lewis Tiffany recognized the clear superiority of the Moore's products and began to commission them to manufacture silverware for his wealthy clientele; and, following the critical acclaim of Moore's products shown by Ball, Tompkins and Black at London's great Crystal Palace Exhibition of 1851, Tiffany convinced the Moores to produce their wares exclusively for Tiffany & Co.

It was about that time that John C. Moore's twenty-four-year-old son succeeded his father and thereby assumed the direction of Tiffany's silver operations. The younger Moore's designs of the 1850s followed, as had his father's, the universally popular Rococo and Classical Revival styles of the period. A visit to the Paris Exposition of 1855 added the Second Empire's Louis XV and Louis XVI Revival styles—augmented by flourishes of Napoleon III neoclassicism—to Moore's, and Tiffany's, design vocabulary.

The following year all this began to change with the publication of England's greatest design guru Owen Jones's celebrated *Grammar of Ornament* (1856). The wealth of information in the catalogue of styles in that very influential work in the history of design would happily redirect Moore's thoughts toward far broader stylistic possibilities. Not least of these was the school of Orientalism inspired by the arts of the

Middle East, with their intricate, colorful, and exotic Islamic patterns.

The disruption of the Civil War called a near halt to silverware production in the first half of the 1860s; however, by the time of the next Paris Exposition in 1867, two years after the conclusion of the war, Moore's silver for the Tiffany & Co. display in Paris would include a "Moresque" tea set (now in the Philadelphia Museum of Art) along with the period's requisite neoclassical designs, and it would win for Tiffany & Co. and America a bronze medal, the first award ever given by a foreign jury for American silverware. The Paris Exposition's theme of Orientalism and the strong presence of the Japanese at that world's fair undoubtedly reinforced Edward C. Moore's penchants for both the Islamic and Japanese revival schools of Near and Far Eastern design, where he was to know no rival.

By 1871 Moore had designed Tiffany's still best-selling "Japanese" flatsilver (renamed "Audubon" during World War II), and by the time of the Philadelphia Centennial Exhibition of 1876, both Moore's and Tiffany's "Persian" and Japanesque silverwares were universally acclaimed and brought Tiffany & Co. gold medals for silverware and for silver inlaid with niello and copper.

Both styles once again triumphed at the Paris Exposition of 1878, where Tiffany's won its first grand prize for silverware, and Charles Lewis Tiffany was named a chevalier of the Legion of Honor. The internationally acclaimed Japanesque silverware created by Moore for the 1878 Paris fair remains America's greatest achievement in silver.

In 1870 Tiffany & Co. had moved to a new and, for the time, palatial building at the southwest corner of Fifteenth Street and Union Square, where Edward C. Moore set up a small applied-arts educational facility popularly called the "Tiffany School." Here apprentices of no less than fifteen years of age learned to draw and model from nature and had access to the extensive and remarkably comprehensive design library that Moore had begun for Tiffany & Co. in the mid-1850s. They also had access to many fine examples of Near Eastern and Oriental art that Moore was steadily assembling into a collection, which was to be unequaled in America. Two of America's most remarkable silver designers, John T. Curran and Paulding Farnham, were trained in Moore's Tiffany School. He also hired other distinguished silversmiths to collaborate on Tiffany silver design, among them Charles T. Grosjean, James Horton Whitehouse, Eugene Julius Soligny, Florent Antoine Heller, and Charles Osborne.

The grand prize for silverware was again awarded to Tiffany & Co. at the Paris Exposition of 1889 for Moore's masterpieces of Saracenic and Japanesque design. Moore, who this time produced the silverware with the collaboration of John T. Curran and Paulding Farnham, amongst others, was given the Legion of Honor by the French government in recognition of his unique contributions to the world of silversmithing. Two years later, on August 2, 1891, Moore's health failed and he died at the age of sixty-four, leaving his early collaborators, James H. Whitehouse, Charles T. Grosjean, and Eugene Soligny, along with the new leadership of his star students John T. Curran and Paulding Farnham, to continue the triumphant progress of Tiffany silver that he had led for forty years.

Although both still in their early thirties, Curran and Farnham were equal to the task, and Tiffany & Co.'s silver displays would win gold medals for its spectacular pieces, including John T. Curran's Magnolia Vase, shown at the Chicago World's Columbian Exposition of 1893, and then yet another grand prize for silver at the Paris Exposition of 1900, where its exhibit included Paulding Farnham's Adams Vase and several extraordinary Native American–influenced showpieces, also by Farnham. Farnham would again win the gold medal for silverware at the 1901 Pan-American Exposition held in Buffalo, New York, with his own jeweled and enameled "Viking" and Saracenic silver, a performance he would repeat at the St. Louis World's Fair of 1904 with his Renaissance Revival silverwares.

Although not attaining the same level of invention, vigor, and originality in their designs and silver crafting as Moore, Curran and Farnham, along with Moore's original collaborators James Whitehouse, Charles Grosjean, Eugene Soligny, and Charles Osborne, made undeniably major contributions to the history of nineteenth-century silver at Tiffany's and in America, and all were undeniably superb craftsmen.

In 1855 James Whitehouse came from his native England, where he was trained as an engraver and designer. In 1858, at twenty-five years of age, he was hired by Moore to work in Tiffany's silver department. That same year Cyrus Field had laid the first transatlantic cable, and Whitehouse began his career at Tiffany's designing a medal to commemorate that event. During the Civil War, he designed many presentation

Designed by John C. and Edward C. Moore in about 1853, this 9¾-inch-tall pitcher is decorated with repoussé-chased cattails and leaves. Its decoration is similar to a stoneware pitcher made in 1835 in England by Ridgway & Co., which specialized in bas-relief floral decorations.

Rococo-revival tea-and-coffee service designed and made by John C. Moore for Tiffany's. The service comprises a coffeepot, teapot, hot-water kettle, creamer, sugar bowl, tea caddy, slop bowl, and ewer (opposite), all decorated with repoussé-chased grapevines and grape clusters. Moore made at least two other tea services in this pattern for Tiffany's competitor Ball, Black & Co.: a five-piece service presented to telegraph company president Marshall Lefferts in June 1850, and a 23½-karat-gold, four-piece service for shipping magnate Edward K. Collins that was exhibited at the Crystal Palace in London in 1851. Moore also made at least two other similar services for Tiffany's: one presented to railroad president Charles F. Pond in 1854 and another for California stagecoach entrepreneur James E. Birch about 1855. The service illustrated here was given to William Backhouse Astor, Jr. and Caroline Webster Schermerhorn on the occasion of their marriage on September 21, 1853. William Astor was a grandson of the fur trader and property investor John Jacob Astor (1763–1848) and a principal heir to the vast New York City real estate holdings that his grandfather had assembled; his bride came from a prosperous "Knickerbocker" family of Dutch descent. Upon learning of the engagement, George Templeton Strong wrote in his diary for June 13, 1853, "Trust the young couple will be able to live on their little incomes together." (*The Diary of George Templeton Strong*, 1952) During the last quarter of the nineteenth century, Mrs. William Astor reigned over "The Four Hundred," the cream of high society in New York and Newport. Her great-grandson sold the tea-and-coffee service at Christie's for $18,700 in June 1993.

An elaborate service of twenty-four pieces commissioned by James E. Birch from Tiffany's and made by John C. Moore, probably in 1855. Birch struck it rich in the California gold rush, operating stagecoach lines with his partner, Frank S. Stevens. The service contains several references to the source of his fortune: two finials are formed as prospectors panning for gold; the soup tureen has a stagecoach finial and bear-head handles; and the tray has engraved scenes of a stagecoach, Sutter's Mill, Sutter's Fort, and a bird's-eye view of the San Francisco waterfront. After he made his fortune, Birch—still in his late twenties—went home to Massachusetts and got married. He then went back to California, sold his business interests, and shipped the proceeds ahead in gold bars. On his return trip in 1857 he was aboard the steamship *Central America* when it was hit by a hurricane off North Carolina and sank on September 12; he was one of 425 passengers who perished. Some time later his former partner, Frank Stevens, visited Birch's widow and young son, Frank Stevens Birch. Stevens and Mrs. Birch eventually married. In 1987–89, salvagers recovered three tons of California gold from the *Central America*'s wreckage.

swords and testimonial pieces for the Northern heroes of the war, and in 1867 he designed one of America's first great horse-racing trophies, the Westchester Cup, for the summer races at Jerome Park. Then in 1874 he designed his most famous piece of silver, the William Cullen Bryant Vase, to commemorate the poet's eightieth birthday on November 3, 1874. This nearly three-foot-high masterpiece of Victorian American silver, completed eighteen months after Bryant's birthday, was presented in a ceremony at New York's Chickering Hall on June 20, 1876; afterwards it was shown to great critical acclaim at the Philadelphia Centennial Exposition that year. Since 1877, when it was donated by William Cullen Bryant, it has been in the collection of the Metropolitan Museum of Art, the first piece of American silver to enter the Metropolitan's collections. In 1884 Whitehouse designed one of the most familiar of all American icons, the still-used obverse of the Great Seal of the United States.

Charles T. Grosjean, a second generation New York silversmith like Edward C. Moore, joined Tiffany & Co. in 1868 at the age of twenty-seven as manager of the company's Prince Street silverworks. He designed a number of Tiffany's flatsilver patterns, including the still-popular "Chrysanthemum" and the "Lap over Edge." Early examples of both were shown at the Paris Exposition of 1878. He created "Wave Edge" four years later, and in 1885 he designed some unique flatware based on explorer-artist George Catlin's illustrations of Native Americans. He has been credited with having significantly contributed to Tiffany's prize-winning silver designs at the

"Neo-grec" five-piece tea and coffee set probably designed by John C. Moore circa 1860–64. The bodies have engraved friezes of horsemen and bands of anthemia, and three of the lids have helmet finials. Many similar pieces were made by English silversmiths in the late 1850s and the 1860s; in this case Moore was inspired by English models. Due to the 30 percent tariff on imported silverware, American silversmiths could easily compete with English makers. Tariff protection often stifles creativity; in this regard the advances in Edward C. Moore's designs in the 1870s are all the more remarkable.

Paris Exposition of 1878, undoubtedly for work on the elaborate 1,250-piece Mackay service made for "Silver Bonanza King" John Mackay and his socialite wife, Marie Louise (Hungerford) Mackay.

The third in this quartet of distinguished early Tiffany silver designers, Eugene Julius Soligny, was a French silversmith who came to New York in his late twenties and joined Tiffany & Co. about 1858 at the age of thirty-six. He was the most highly skilled chaser, or modeler, of silver in America, and he modeled both Whitehouse's Bryant Vase and the Jerome Park trophy, as well as such remarkable works as his own vigorously sculptural Comanche Cup of 1873.

The fourth, but by no means the least distinguished, of Tiffany's star nineteenth-century silver designers was Charles Osborne. In 1871 the twenty-three-year-old Osborne went to work for Whiting, a competitor in the silver business, where he quickly rose to become head designer. Attracted, however, by

Edward C. Moore's genius as both educator and master, and by the broader horizons for his talents offered by Tiffany's as the recognized leader in silver design (Tiffany's having just won the grand prize for silver at the Paris Exposition), Osborne resigned from Whiting on November 15, 1878 and began a nine-year association with Moore and Tiffany's before returning to Whiting in 1887, again as their head designer.

His work at Tiffany's showed the prodigiously adroit handling of floral and aquatic design, along with his penchant for vigorous, spiraling compositions. Under Edward C. Moore's direction and with his inspiration, he broadened his reach in design with a curious mixture of Islamic and Orientalist themes. The result was a unique contribution of high-style Victorian masterpieces, which included numerous yachting trophies, the magnificent floral tea service made in 1884–86 and shown to universal critical acclaim at the Paris Exposition of 1889, and an atypical group of Tiffany silver distinguished by spirals of chased "pearling" mixed with the seaweed and sea creatures or the flowers, such as wild roses, dogwood, and Oriental poppies, that Osborne loved so much.

In the nineteenth century Tiffany & Co. was the unchallenged master of American silver design and craftsmanship, and it retained that distinction during the twentieth century, beginning with the richly eclectic works of Paulding Farnham, and continuing through the stylishly abstract, organic forms of Elsa Peretti's contemporary silver. Along the way in the twentieth century, designs in silver by Louis Comfort Tiffany and Frank Lloyd Wright, as well as by lesser-known, but all in their own way remarkable, silver designers such as Albert Southwick, Arthur Barney, and Van Day Truex, have brightened the spectacular history of Tiffany silver. That Tiffany & Co., remains America's greatest silver maker at the outset of the twenty-first century is due to the solid foundation laid down by Edward C. Moore nearly a century-and-a-half ago.

Moore's quest for the highest levels of quality of design, craftsmanship, and material has remained a constant throughout Tiffany's history and has led its name to be synonymous with "quality."

Styles have evolved from Victorian Realism and Orientalism, to Impressionist Japanism, and continued to Art Nouveau, Art Deco, Modernism, and Post-Modernism, but the quest for excellence, as well as the quest for a truly American Tiffany style, has always been at the heart of Tiffany silver.

Covered water pitcher in the form of a barrel designed by John C. and Edward C. Moore for Tiffany's circa 1859. This was a popular style in silver in the late 1850s. The Moores made a punch bowl in the form of a ship's water keg and a wine cooler in the form of a ship's bucket awarded to the winners of the New York Yacht Club's Ocean Regatta on June 24–26, 1858.

EDWARD C. MOORE

Silver-and-gilt wine cooler decorated with birds and branches designed by Edward C. Moore circa 1875. The maple leaf and seed border was reused by Eugene J. Soligny on the "Night" salver he designed for the 1878 Paris Exposition (see page 132). Soligny may well have executed the chasing on this piece.

Edward C. Moore was without doubt the greatest silversmith America produced in the last half of the nineteenth century. His designs for Tiffany & Co. won the grand prizes for silver at the Paris Expositions of both 1878 and 1889; and, at the 1889 Exposition he was made a Chevalier of the Legion of Honor.

The great Parisian dealer, writer, and collector Siegfried Bing (1838–1905), whose style-setting Paris shop gave its name to the Art Nouveau movement, cited Moore along with fellow Americans Louis Comfort Tiffany and John La Farge as outstanding artist-designers of their time who Europe "would have been proud to possess." Commenting on the widespread and unprecedented enthusiasm for silver design generated by Moore's Japanesque silverwares at the 1878 Exposition, Bing wrote that "This sudden resurgence was due to the clairvoyance of a man whose country should forever enshrine him in grateful memory; Edward C. Moore, artistic director of the famous Tiffany & Co., was one of the first to comprehend the real value of the treasures just emerging from the Orient."

Quite unlike the son of his employer Charles Lewis Tiffany—the flamboyant and ever publicity-hungry Louis Comfort Tiffany—Moore was, like his employer, almost pathologically reticent. He granted no interviews and refrained from writing about his work, resulting today in a near-total eclipse of his reputation as "Prince of Silversmiths." The title was conferred upon him in an article that appeared in the August 29, 1891, issue of the *Illustrated American* about four weeks after his untimely death at sixty-four. It concisely summed up Moore's preeminent position in the decorative arts of America and silver design: "The late Edward C. Moore was easily the foremost silversmith in the United States. It is largely due to his skill and industry that American silverware has reached a degree of perfection that makes it celebrated all over the world. He practically developed a new industry here: but modest and retiring, almost morbidly adverse to publicity of any kind, he passed through life without assuming in the eyes of the general public the credit he so well deserved. In the words of his warm friend, Mr. S. P. Avery, the world will never fully know the loss it met in the death of Mr. Moore, and what he did for the industrial arts will never be fully told."

Japanesque bud vase, 6⅜ inches tall. It has applied copper-and-silver panels of Japanese scenes, applied silver leaves, a gold butterfly, and a moth with *mokume* wings. (*Mokume*, the Japanese word for wood grain, is a mixed-metal laminate.) The shape was called "ten pin" in Tiffany's pattern book, and it was made in several variations.

Moore's early work of the 1850s and early 1860s found favor with Charles Lewis Tiffany's monied New York clientele for its clarity of form and for its superb craftsmanship, if not for any great originality of design. Immediately following the Civil War, however, a personal style began to emerge in Moore's first designs, based on Near Eastern and Far Eastern rather than Western European arts.

Encouraged by the bronze medal awarded Tiffany & Co. for his silverware at the Paris Exposition of 1867 and stimulated by the increased interest in the arts of both Islam and Japan that the exposition launched, Moore sharpened his focus on silver design inspired by those cultures.

It is not possible to precisely chronicle Edward C. Moore's career between the Paris Exposition of 1867 and the Philadelphia Centennial Exposition nine years later, nor in later years, for that matter. However, a combination of facts and educated guesses sketch an acceptable picture of Moore's collecting, professorial, and designing activities.

From one of Moore's sketchbooks dated "Paris—July 26, 1855," a month before his twenty-eighth birthday, we know that he had been sent to Paris to visit the French Second Empire's first exposition in the company of Tiffany's highly design-educated partner, Gideon F. T. Reed, and to gather design ideas. It was also recorded that while there he visited several French design schools to study the workings of a Parisian applied-arts education with a view to establishing a design school at Tiffany & Co.

No record exists, but it is more than probable that he visited the London Exposition of 1862, and that five years later he again visited the French capital, by then at the peak of Second Empire splendor. He may well have been present on that historic afternoon of July 1 when the prizes for the exposition of 1867 were distributed with great pomp and ceremony in the Palace of Industry, in the presence of the Emperor Napoleon III and the Empress Eugénie. To the astonishment of all present, an American firm, Tiffany & Co., won the bronze medal for Moore's silver, the first time an American company had been awarded a medal by a foreign jury.

Moore is known to have made frequent visits to Europe, where he dedicated his time not only to studying the applied arts of Europe, Islam, and the Orient in the museums of both London and Paris, where Tiffany maintained branch stores, but also to amassing the extraordinary collection of Islamic and Oriental art objects that would inspire his works of

Portrait of Edward C. Moore by an unknown artist circa 1889, when he was made a chevalier of the French Legion of Honor. In the background is a pair of Egyptian doors inlaid with geometric ivory patterns by Mamluk craftsmen, probably in the late fourteenth century. Moore bequeathed the doors to the Metropolitan Museum of Art, and they are now in the Museum's Islamic Galleries.

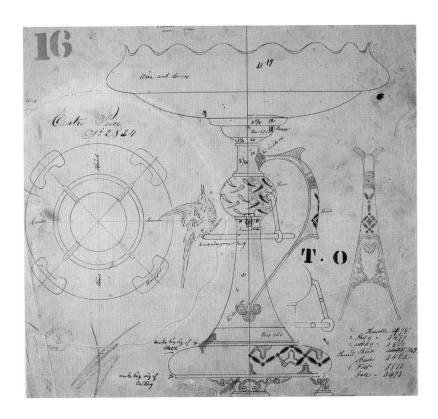

ABOVE:

⚓ Enameling drawing for a Japanesque tea caddy designed by Edward C. Moore in the 1870s. Preliminary sketches of these storks are in Moore's sketchbook. The background pattern of Chinese clouds appears on the borders of several Tiffany trays, including the one illustrated on page 146. ⚓

RIGHT:

⚓ Drawing for a Japanesque centerpiece bowl ("holds 6 pints") decorated with "iris and daisies." The sheet is stamped "Dec 5, 1871," the year Edward C. Moore's "Japanese" (now called "Audubon") flatware was introduced, showing that he began designing Japanesque hollowware earlier than most authors have stated. The base for this piece (#3484) was used again on Moore's much-published Brush Pot Vase on page 28. ⚓

Japanesque and Saracenic silver design for Tiffany's and would also be pivotal to his educational program for apprentices in his Tiffany School. Moore certainly did not reveal his sources, but his acquaintance with noted dealers of Orientalist art, such as Landros and Company in London and Siegfried Bing in Paris, would suggest that he bought from both.

The New York newspaper *The Sun* mentioned amongst Moore's objects of Orientalist art an Indian metal plate "damascened in arabesques...from the Vienna Exposition of 1873," indicating that Moore probably visited that exposition too, where Tiffany & Co. exhibited a splendid array of presentation silver (a good portion of it now in the collection of the Art

Institute of Chicago). He was certainly in Europe the following year, 1874, as the noted American art dealer Samuel P. Avery mentioned in his diaries; he met Moore in London on July 17 and again in Paris on July 26.

England's design guru of the time, Christopher Dresser, worked with Landros and Company, and it must have been on Moore's 1874 London visit that he formulated the plan to have Dresser buy for Tiffany & Co. as well as for Landros on his next visit to Japan, which would take place two years later.

His first important Japanesque design was his now-renowned "Audubon" flatsilver (patented on April 18, 1871), with its exotic bird amongst unconventional branches, leaves, and flowers. This was followed in 1872 by the more elaborate "Vine" pattern featuring a stippled background setting off hanging gourds and tendrils sculpted in relief; they would be typical of Moore's more mature Japanesque style six years later.

A drawing in the Tiffany Archives for an elaborate Japanesque six-pint punch bowl centerpiece with two sculpted exotic birds perched between two elaborately pierced and patterned divided handles (and sitting on the same bulbous pierced Japanesque diaperwork base that was reused later for the spider-and-dragonfly "brush-holder" vase now in the Brooklyn Museum) is dated December 5, 1871. It therefore affirms that the development of Japanesque hollowware was concomitant with the appearance of Japanesque flatsilver at Tiffany & Co., and that the development of the Japanesque style must have begun in the last years of the 1860s.

The broken chevron pattern entwined with small undulating flowered vines of the Japanese-inspired "Daisy Work" that ornaments a tea set (now in the New-York Historical Society) appeared at about the same time. It is worth noting that the drawings for the "Daisy Work" tea set are dated October 30, 1872, and that their truncated disk forms and their clear, angular structure further indicate their author's more-than-passing familiarity with the bare simplicity, angularity, and revealed structure of Christopher Dresser's own Japaniste designs.

By the time of the Philadelphia Centennial Exposition of 1876, the inlaying of metallic black niello and of copper had been added to Moore's vocabulary in Japanese- and Islamic-inspired silverwares. Unlike his more three-dimensional later work, the Japanesque tea set and vases seen in an 1876 illustration indicate that the Japanesque wares shown in Philadelphia

Japanesque tea caddy decorated with pike designed by Edward C. Moore circa 1877. This model with an alternate décor was shown at the 1878 Paris Exposition. The London *Spectator* commented on Tiffany's Japanesque wares at the Exposition, "The articles made in the developed Japanese style were marked by simplicity and boldness of form, and entire independence from the mouldings, flutings, and other extra refinements which make up the Renaissance and Louis XVI style.... This decoration was rendered more varied and attractive by the use of metallic colours, the natural ones of gold, silver, platinum, and the artificial produced by alloys, while chemical processes have also been drawn upon. This decorative colouring is also derived from Japanese art, but has been so developed by Tiffany & Co., through the aid of chemistry and machinery, that they now possess a greater variety, and in some instances, finer qualities of colour than the Japanese." (September 21, 1878)

Edward C. Moore took the cylindrical form and the spider-and-dragonfly decoration of the upper portion of this 9 ⅜-inch-tall vase from a bronze Japanese brush pot in his collection, which he bequeathed to the Metropolitan Museum of Art. Charles H. Carpenter wrote, "The Japanese bronze has a pebbly, sand cast background which the Tiffany piece translates as a hand-hammered surface. But the cast Tiffany base (whose form derives from Chinese and Japanese carved wood pedestal stands) is far more elegant. The overall effect of the Japanese bronze is one of a rather casually made production of folk art, while the Tiffany vase has an almost jewel-like perfection. The Tiffany piece is far more carefully made, more studied, and is exquisitely finished. This is not a value judgment, but only a description of how Tiffany used one of their Japanese models." ("Tiffany silver in the Japanese style," *The Connoisseur*, January 1979)

Small (9⅜-inch-wide) Japanesque spiderweb tray with a dragonfly and a miniature maple leaf designed by Edward C. Moore for the 1878 Paris Exposition. The spiderweb motif was taken from the nineteenth-century bronze Japanese brush pot that he also used as the basis for the Brush Pot Vase on the opposite page.

had quite flat surfaces, depending only on engraving and inlaid niello and copper for their patterns.

The more sculptural qualities of the 1871 exotic bird punch bowl/centerpiece would be revived immediately after the Philadelphia Centennial. Saracenic (first termed "Persian") pieces for Philadelphia were elaborately hand chased with scrolling, serrated leaves, and rosette flowers inspired by the patterns of sixteenth- and seventeenth-century Iznik ceramics in Moore's collection or with other stylized exotic flora of Middle Eastern inspiration.

Between 1876 and the Paris Exposition of 1878, radical advances were made in Moore's Tiffany Japanesque silverwares. Smooth backgrounds were replaced by a revolutionary use of *martelé*, or hammered, finishes, beginning in late 1876.

Although used occasionally prior to 1876, applied three-dimensional flora and fauna that ultimately included insects, fish, crustaceans, reptiles, assorted vines, flowers, and gourds appeared in abundance a few months later in early 1877. The arrival at Tiffany & Co. of thousands of decorative arts objects collected by Christopher Dresser on his aforementioned 1876–77 voyage to Japan has been largely credited for inspiring these, along with the use of mixed metal elements.

Moore never commented on Dresser's collections and their influence on Tiffany design; but, the coincidence of date strongly suggests that Edward C. Moore and his associates had gathered considerable new design knowledge from Dresser's early-1877 shipment.

In any case, by the time of the Paris Exposition of 1878, Moore's Japanesque style was at its height. The splendid exhibit of Japanesque Tiffany silver with its undulating volumetric forms, its soft, hammered surfaces, asymmetries, applied ornaments, inlaid and mixed metals—all used with an extraordinary grace, harmony, and restraint for the period—won Tiffany & Co. the grand prize for silverware and a gold medal for Moore, awarded again in the Champs-Élysées's Palace of Industry, but this time by French President Marshal Mac-Mahon together with the Prince of Wales on October 21.

Moore's magnificent Japanesque wares were the pinnacle of his achievement and remain the greatest works in the history of American silver. Still, with a gold medal for himself and the grand prize for his silver designs, Moore maintained his silence. He made no recorded comments, even after being covered with such glory for his long, hard, and brilliant efforts.

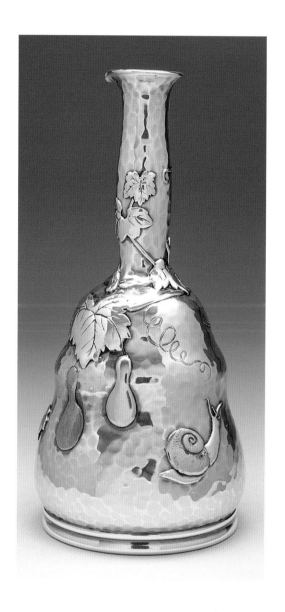

⟿ The rim of this small (5¾-inch-tall) and exquisite Japanesque bud vase has a lip, indicating that it was based on a sake bottle. Many of Edward C. Moore's Japanesque pieces (coffeepots, for example) were made for purposes unknown in Japan at the time, and this is one of the few Japanesque pieces whose actual form was Japanese. That being said, Japanese sake bottles (and teapots) are almost always ceramic, not silver: Moore's Japanesque enterprise was the adaptation of Japanese techniques and aesthetics to useful objects traditionally made of silver in the West. ⟿

◢ Japanesque tea-and-coffee set decorated with birds and branches designed by Edward C. Moore circa 1871–72. ◣

◢ Japanesque salt dish set decorated with birds and branches, designed by Edward C. Moore circa 1871–72. ◣

Flask with birds and branches
designed by Edward C. Moore
circa 1871–72.

The French critic Émile Bergerat gently chided him for this in his illustrated *Masterpieces of Art at the Universal Exposition* (Paris, 1878): "But, if there exists an American artist capable of conceiving the delicious patterns of the pitchers, cups, vases, and match safes that I was shown at the Exposition, I advise him to sign his work. He will be famous in Paris within eight days." Moore, of course, did not sign his works—no Tiffany designer did—and he must have made it abundantly clear to the press that he wished his anonymity respected.

There was, of course, no lack of praise piled on his Japanesque wares.

The U.S. Commissioner to the 1878 Exposition, the Honorable Richard C. McCormick wrote in *The North American Review* (July 1879): "The articles made in the developed Japanese style were marked by simplicity and boldness of form, and entire independence from the moldings, flutings, and other extra refinements which make up the Renaissance and Louis XVI style. They were decorated in the manner taught by the Japanese, which is an outgrowth of their subtle appreciation of contrast and effect, and their love of nature, which, with its simple and truthful application of plants, blossoms, flowers, and other natural objects, stands in marked contrast to the decorative mannerisms prevailing in Europe. . . .The specimens of work made of the new metal formed by the lamination of all the noble metals and their alloys astonished even the Japanese, from whom the method was learned, many articles having been purchased by them; their chief commissioner having bought one of the principal specimens for his Government."

A *New York Herald* cable dispatch (May 12, 1878) noted: "Tiffany's exhibit is attracting universal attention for beauty and originality of design, and perfection of workmanship. Nothing of the kind in the Exhibition approaches their models." *The New York World* Paris correspondent added (July 11, 1878): "Now the Japanese work has become the rage on this side, and the Japanese themselves have been the first to show their appreciation of it by ordering specimens of it for a native museum. TIFFANY & CO., it seems, with their superior mechanical appliances, have carried the manufacture beyond the power or even the conception of its Asiatic inventors."

Amid all the newspaper coverage, only *The New York Commercial Advertiser* (September 27, 1878) revealed the designer's name: "There can be no doubt that in everything concerning the silver department (apart from the general enterprise of the firm), the greatest credit is due to Mr. E. C. Moore. An old silver-smith by trade, and the son of a widely-known silversmith, he combines natural abilities with an experience of nearly fifty years' hard work. From morning till night he is at the shop, super-intending every detail of the work; and when the factory is closed he is collecting and selecting models and designs in bric-à-brac shops, in libraries, or in private collections."

Moore's collaborator Christopher Dresser showed just satisfaction in his own contributions to the Japanesque Tiffany style when he wrote his congratulations to the firm: "I cannot refrain from expressing to you the pleasure that I have derived from the contemplation of your exhibit in the present Paris Exhibition. No silversmith, that I know, has made the progress in art as applied to their industry in the last few years that you have—indeed, the rapidity of your advancement has astonished many of my art friends as well as myself. After much consideration, I cannot help thinking that—judged by the exhibits of Paris—you occupy the proud position of being the first silversmiths of the world."

Teapot from the "Daisy Work" Japanesque tea set designed by Edward C. Moore, made from a drawing dated October 30, 1872. Its flat, space-saving shape shows the influence of the great English designer Christopher Dresser's pared-down utilitarianism.

OPPOSITE, BOTTOM:
Sketch of a starfish by Edward C. Moore circa 1878, a rare example of his drawing from nature. It is a key to the understanding of the organic, fleshy, undulating handles of Moore's Japanesque silver after 1878.

Two Japanesque tea caddies designed by Edward C. Moore circa 1878. Both are very similar to models with niello-and-copper decoration shown at the 1878 Paris Exposition, seen in the archival photograph at left. The caddy on the right has a gold-lacquered Japanese ivory plaque on the front, and its lid has a handle inspired by the work of the English designer Christopher Dresser. The ivory plaque was probably part of a shipment of thousands of examples of Japanese arts and crafts purchased by Dresser in 1876–77 for Tiffany & Co. on Moore's instructions and auctioned by Tiffany's in New York. Moore used some of these pieces as inspiration for the collection of Japanesque silverware shown by Tiffany's at the 1878 Paris Exposition.

Tiffany's 1878 archival photograph of Japanesque pieces made for the Paris Exposition. It shows a coffee set comprising a pot and two mugs decorated with fish and reeds, a gourd-shaped tray, a water pitcher, a sugar bowl, two spoons, and a knife rest. This informal arrangement is imbued with the period's "artistic" sensibility, which stood in opposition to the extravagance of the Mackay service that Tiffany's exhibited in Paris at the same time. Siegfried Bing, the dealer in Oriental art whose Paris shop La Maison de l'Art Nouveau gave the movement its name, wrote in 1895,

> Many of those amateurs [connoisseurs] whose interest extends to all areas of art will still remember their surprise on seeing, at the Exposition of 1878, several examples of the metalwork of the most extraordinary quality. Although not intrinsically original in concept—their decorative principles were taken directly from the Japanese—their borrowed elements were so ingeniously transposed to serve their new function as to become the equivalent of new discoveries. In any case, these useful objects were attractive, not least because they had ceased to embody the constant reincarnation of our own traditional forms, however charming, whose interest had long palled with repetition. This sudden resurgence was due to the clairvoyance of a man whose country should forever enshrine him in grateful memory; Edward C. Moore (born 1827) the artistic director of Tiffany & Co. (*Artistic America, Tiffany Glass, and Art Nouveau*)

Little since has been written on Moore's great contribution toward modernizing American design in the decorative arts through the influence of his Japanesque wares.

Japonisme was, of course, not his invention. Following Commodore Matthew Perry and the American Navy's opening of Japan on March 31, 1854, trade agreements were signed within the next two years with the United States, France, England, Russia, and the Netherlands.

Japanese woodblock prints (which exerted an incalculably great influence on Western art) as well as Japanese textiles, ceramics, bronzes, and lacquers soon followed and were avidly collected, most notably by the Impressionist painters in France, whom they pointed in a whole new direction in art with their simplification and decorative abstraction of the world and with their obvious total disregard for illusionism, perspective, or the mimetic realism as practiced by academic Western art. In short, with their refreshing and liberating vision of a world decoratively composed of bright colors and stylishly bold patterns cast against clear, flat, horizonless, and shadowless backgrounds, they were just what enlightened Western artists in search of modernism were looking for. They were also what Moore looked for.

Japonisme's first effects were seen in Impressionist paintings, but the French ceramic designer Félix Bracquemond is generally credited with introducing Japonisme to the decorative arts. He bought a copy of the famous woodcut sketchbook *Manga* by the Japanese artist Hokusai (1760–1849) in 1857 and ten years later decorated a stoneware table service with motifs appropriated from Hokusai for a well-known Paris ceramics dealer, François Eugène Rousseau. The service was exhibited at the Paris Exposition of 1867 where Moore most likely saw it. On his collecting trips to Paris, Moore would clearly have visited François Rousseau's ceramics shop either on his own or been taken there by Tiffany's Paris partner, Gideon F. T. Reed, and may well have purchased Japanese art objects from Rousseau for his own and for the Tiffany School's collections of prototypes. At some point he also purchased several copies of Hokusai's *Manga*. Two remain today in the Tiffany Archives.

Moore's late-1860s sketchbook (also in the Tiffany Archives) affirms that about 1867 he began designing in a Japoniste style. This new direction could itself have well been the result of a visit to the 1867 Paris Exposition, as there is no evidence that his designs before that date showed any Japanese influences. For ten years afterward, he devoted his best efforts to distill-

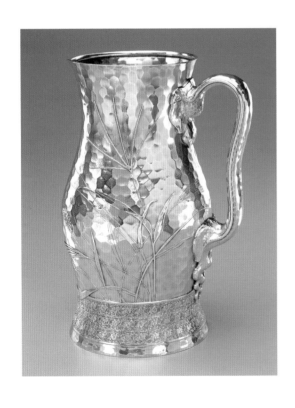

Pitcher with repoussé prairie grass designed by Edward C. Moore in 1878; the sparsely ornamented hand-hammering is characteristic of many of his later Japanesque pieces.

ing the principles of Japanese art into his own dazzlingly jewel-like version of Japonisme with its so beautifully clear, simple, and perfect harmony of forms, patterns, and materials, which brought such high honors to Tiffany & Co. and America at the 1878 Paris Exposition.

The development of Edward C. Moore's Orientalist or, as he baptized it, "Saracenic" style, although begun before 1867, ran more or less parallel to the Japanesque. The style would not, however, reach its full height until the time of the Paris Exposition of 1889, when it would again merit Tiffany & Co. the grand prize for silverware and see Moore's genius recognized by the French, who made him a chevalier of the Legion of Honor.

The Japanesque style remained immensely popular throughout the 1880s and evolved significantly, as did the Saracenic style, which was enriched by the addition of a palette of brilliantly colored enamels. These brought a new and painterly quality to Moore's designs, which the older niello and copper inlays shown in Philadelphia in 1876 had not provided.

Form, as well as surface treatment, became increasingly complex as the style evolved, and as the simplicity of Iznik ceramic patternings was gradually dissolved in the intricacies of Persian and Mughal trellises, arabesques, and flowers. These intracacies, many of them inspired by Owen Jones's *The Grammar of Ornament*, led Moore in a direction quite opposite to England's Arts and Crafts Movement, whose leader, William Morris, often denounced Owen Jones's design teachings. Moore may well have taken this path deliberately to clearly set Tiffany's apart from the Arts and Crafts Movement.

The Illustrated American's August 29,1891, article on Moore's work titled "A Prince of Silversmiths" reviewed the enameled silver of 1889 with due enthusiasm:

> His great work for this exposition was Saracenic both in form and decoration. This Saracenic was the pride of his life, and to it he gave his undivided attention in preparation for the Exposition of 1889. The ware is Saracenic chiefly in the form. In the decorations Mr. Moore introduced many new features heretofore foreign to metalwork.
>
> Enameling on metals was another one of Mr. Moore's favorite studies, his efforts being devoted to overcoming the glazy and glittering effects so common in Russian and Persian silverware. How well he succeeded may be seen on the beautiful work in the Saracenic ware. Orchids of many varieties are reproduced with true fidelity as to colors and every minute detail, from the stem to the tip of the leaves, in hard, dull enamels, and bear the imprint of the most marvelous delicacy and rare genius in their treatment. In some of the pieces the effect of the enameling is enriched by pierced or open work, oxidizing or stone-finish.

Two Japanesque water pitchers. Left: this 7¾-inch-tall pitcher designed by Edward C. Moore has a French import control mark indicating that it may have been shown at the 1878 Paris Exposition. It is applied with copper maple leaves on yellow metal stems, a leaf with a grasshopper, a dragonfly, two butterflies, two *mokume* gourds, and one gourd in *sentoku* (a colored Japanese alloy). Right: copper pitcher made between 1891 and 1902, after Moore's death but from a circa 1878 Moore design. The 8½-inch-tall body is engraved with aquatic plants and applied with silver dragonflies and a fish swimming through reeds; the handle has a silver frog. Its base, rim, and interior are silver.

OPPOSITE:

Japanesque hot-water jug, 7¼ inches tall, decorated with a copper-and-yellow-metal wisteria with hanging seed pods, a *mokume* butterfly, a copper and brass butterfly, and a bug on the handle.

≈ Hammered silver punch bowl, 15¾ inches in diameter, designed by Edward C. Moore in 1882. The foot has applied copper dragonflies and flowers. One hundred years after the bowl was made, Tiffany & Co. gave it to the Dallas Museum of Fine Arts to commemorate the opening of the firm's Dallas branch. ≈

OPPOSITE, TOP:
≈ After-dinner coffee set with applied copper and gold, designed by Edward C. Moore circa 1878. The sugar bowl is decorated with lotuses, the creamer with millet, and the 7½-inch-tall coffeepot with a flowering vine. ≈

OPPOSITE, BOTTOM:
≈ Japanesque tray, 10¾ inches long, designed by Edward C. Moore. The handle is red metal, the dragonfly is copper with gold wings, and the gourd is gold. The tendrils of the vine show Moore's direct influence on the Art Nouveau movement. Many versions of this popular tray were made; one was shown at the 1878 Paris Exposition. ≈

The Saracenic wares of 1889 were to be the final flowering of Edward C. Moore's great genius as a silversmith. He compiled in them all that he loved in Islamic art and all that he had learned through collecting, studying, and teaching the art of intricate geometric and floral patternings.

As he employed the vocabulary of Japanese art, Moore used the vocabulary of the arts of Islam to articulate a totally fresh and new design statement of his own. Again there was perfection in the highly complex harmony of form, decoration, and materials, and the familiar jewel-like quality; in the deft shifts and transitions of materials and décor; and in the perfect proportion of form dominating the orchestration of colors and patterns.

The Japanesque style had been Moore's love affair with Impressionism; this was his passionate flirtation with Art Nouveau, and it would have to be carried on by others: by his sometime student Louis Comfort Tiffany and his apprentice John T. Curran.

Exhausted by the work he put into the silver for the 1889 Exposition, Moore's health began to fail and he died on August 2, 1891, at Hastings-on-Hudson, New York. At sixty-four, he was "a man whose country should forever enshrine him in grateful memory" (Siegfried Bing, 1878) as one of its greatest decorative artists.

Japanesque tray with a swallow and wisteria vines designed by Edward C. Moore circa 1878.

Circa 1878 photograph from the Tiffany Archives showing a mixed-metal Japanesque tray and water pitcher decorated with trout and grasses. Designed by Edward C. Moore and shown at the 1878 Paris Exposition.

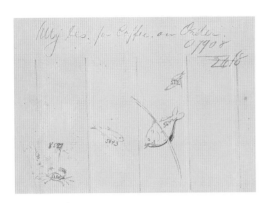

◈ Edward C. Moore's circa 1878 drawing for a Japanesque coffeepot. ◈

◈ Hammered-silver Japanesque flask with a fish inspired by Katsushika Hokusai's *Manga*. ◈

Hammered-silver Japanesque tea set designed by Edward C. Moore circa 1880; the teapot has the same fish and reed decoration as the flask on page 45. The finials on the lids of the teapot and sugar bowl are jade. The squared shapes, surprisingly modern for Tiffany silver of the time, show the influence of Moore's friend Christopher Dresser.

LEFT:

Café-au-lait set designed by Edward C. Moore circa 1880. The copper-on-silver bodies have applied turtles and bamboo leaves, and finials in the form of frogs.

OPPOSITE:

Japanesque water pitcher designed by Edward C. Moore circa 1878, 7¾ inches tall. Silver laminated with copper and decorated with silver and gold irises, dragonflies, and fish.

The copper ground of this three-piece coffee set makes it among the most striking examples of Edward C. Moore's Japanesque silverware. Each piece is decorated with silver dragonflies, and their bases are inlaid with copper and gold geometric motifs. The 8¾-inch-tall coffeepot has *mokume* clouds on the body and *mokume* speckles on the spout and handle; its finial is a dragonfly. A matching coffee set is at the Detroit Institute of Arts.

Japanesque vase, circa 1878, designed by Edward C. Moore.

Japanesque vase designed by Edward C. Moore circa 1880, 10¾ inches tall. The copper body is covered with pale gray enamel and has applied silver, copper, and brass decoration; the interior is silver plated. This side of the vase has silver irises and a jumping carp; the other side has brass bamboo stalks, silver lily pads, a bee, and a dragonfly. It is now at the Charles Hosmer Morse Museum of American Art in Winter Park, Florida. An identical vase sold at Christie's for $7,150 in January 1988.

The Conglomerate Vase was widely recognized as the most important work of Japanesque silver shown at the 1878 Paris Exposition, and it has subsequently been acclaimed as the most important work of nineteenth-century American silver. The 20¼-inch-tall vase has the traditional ovoid *Mei-ping* form and is decorated in niello, copper, gold, and *sentoku* with Japanese maple leaves and seedpods, paulownia leaves and vines, gourds, flowers, flower buds, a butterfly, and a dragonfly; it also has asymmetrical panels of *mokume*. Tiffany's had been producing Japanesque hollowware since late 1871 or 1872, and by the time of the 1878 Paris Exposition, Moore and his associates were designing and producing works that have never been surpassed. The French author Emile Bergerat pondered whether they might have been made by Japanese workers: "Certain motifs seem to me such extraordinary imitations of the Japanese manner that I am struck by a doubt as to their originality. Can it be that Tiffany's does not employ Japanese workers in New-York! That seems at all events a very nasty idea. I submit the problem to the sagacity of the jury without charging the verdict, for until now the Japanese have hardly left the sacred shadow of Fujiyama. But, if there exists an American artist capable of conceiving the charming motifs of the pitchers, cups, vases, and match-holders shown me at the Exposition, I counsel him to sign his work. He will be celebrated in Paris in eight hours." (*Les chefs-d'oeuvres d'art à l'Exposition Universelle*, 1878) Bergerat's musings account for the stories—all originating in France—that Tiffany's employed Japanese metalworkers, which it did not. The artist, of course, was Edward C. Moore, but he had to content himself with a gold medal while company president Charles L. Tiffany was made a chevalier of the French Legion of Honor. The Conglomerate Vase was purchased at the exposition by John T. Martin, a collector of Barbizon School paintings, who displayed it prominently in the picture gallery of his house at 28 Pierrepont Street in Brooklyn. The vase sold at Sotheby's on January 20, 1998 for $585,500.

A very fine 9¾-inch-tall Japanesque vase designed by Edward C. Moore, probably for the 1878 Paris Exposition. Its decoration includes a gold-and-copper dragonfly, a Japanese mask, purplish metal wisteria, and free-form shapes of niello, enamel, and *mokume*. A Japanese newspaper reporter wrote that Tiffany's had "very beautiful examples of our 'mokume' metal which is, I am told, fruit of their hard study and work for many years. Thus I see in metal works as well as in pottery our art so much imitated & admired & it is to be sure very pleasing to see, but at the same time it is to be feared most also. . . . So I warn our manufacturers at home to note these facts & in future to be more and more studious and enterprising." Tiffany's "List of Purchasers" at the 1878 Exposition included "Mr. K. Wakai, Japan" and "Mr. Minoda Chojiro, Japan."

✎ Tiffany's silversmiths used a more complex version of *mokume* for the most widely discussed work in silver at the 1889 Paris Exposition, the 32-inch-tall Laminate Vase, priced at $5,000. The Paris *Herald* reported that the vase's body was "—made of Kokomo [sic], or laminated or mixed metals, as it has been termed. Some ten years ago it was believed by Europeans that this metal would remain a Japanese secret, but Messrs. Tiffany & Co., after a long series of arduous experiments, succeeded in producing it and manufacturing this splendidly perfect example. . . . [It] is composed of fine gold, fine silver, *shakado, sedo,* and *shibuci,* the latter three being Japanese alloys, all folded together in a block of twenty-four layers; this block was then twisted and rolled out under the pressure of a 200-ton roller, and, finally, the large piece was backed with sterling silver, rounded and joined. The difficult process of folding, hammering, and rolling is only accomplished by the greatest care, it being necessary that each metal should stretch and flow alike. The sheet of metal being prepared, the slow and laborious process follows of hammering it into form, during which the metals have to be kept compact and connected in one piece." (September 30, 1889) A *New York Times* reporter commented: "This has never been done in Japan to this extent, and on the day of my visit, a group of Japanese were being initiated into the deeper mysteries of the art. Judging by their gestures and . . . enthusiasm . . . they must have been both highly pleased and astonished." (June 30, 1889) Edward C. Moore's family acquired the Laminate Vase. His grandson, Louis de Bébian Moore (Tiffany's president from 1940 to 1955), removed its neck and base when he had it made into a lamp. Louis Moore's two daughters gave the lamp—made from the vase's central section—to the Cooper-Hewitt Museum in 1976. ✎

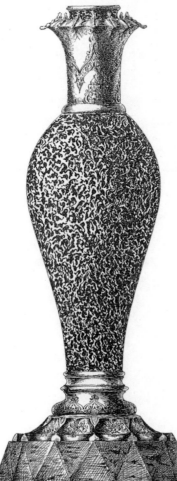

THE JEWELERS' WEEKLY.   47

tusks, spring from the silver base, which is chased with groupings of elephants. The vessel stands upon elephants' feet. Upon the front of the body of the cup is a flute player in relief. This is one of the most exquisite articles in the exhibit and is the subject of one of our illustrations.

The buffalo loving cup is one of the most thoroughly American and, to the mind of the writer, one of the most imposing pieces in the collection. It is about 18 inches in height, the body being of smooth, stone finished silver, inlaid with copper and niello in designs obtained from blanket and wigwam decoration by North American Indians. The handles are representations of the horns of buffaloes and are of burnished silver, forming an effective contrast with the less bright body of the cup. The lower part of the body is decorated with bas-reliefs of Indian dancers, and the whole stands upon feet in imitation of the hoofs of buffaloes, buffalo heads magnificently executed, surmounting them where they are joined to the base of the cup.

The most remarkable triumph of Tiffany & Co. is perhaps their laminated vase. It is made of laminated metals of contrasting colors and is a finished, difficult and interesting piece of workmanship. The body of the vase is composed of fine gold, fine silver, shakado, sedo and shi-hie-chi, the

last named three being Japanese alloys. These metals were all folded together in twenty-four layers and backed by sterling silver. The difficult process of folding, rolling and hammering can only be accomplished by the exercise of the greatest care, it being absolutely necessary that all the five kinds of metal shall stretch and flow alike. The sheet of metal once prepared, the slow and laborious process of hammering it into form follows, and during its execution the several metals must not be separated or allowed to spring away from one another in the slightest degree. The base and neck, both of silver, were attached to the body of the vase after its completion. This wonderful vase is the largest piece ever made of mixed or laminated metals. Fine gold worth $1,200 was used in its composition, in addition to silver and other expensive metals. The price of this vase is $5,000. Its height is 32 inches.

A loving cup of exceptional beauty. is 9½ inches high and 9 inches in diameter. It is strictly Saracenic in form and decoration. It seems to grow from a richly carved rosette beneath its body into six large swells and becomes round at the top. The decoration consists of large flowers near the bottom, chased and enameled and connected by graceful Saracenic lines with the enameled bosses and flowers at the top of the cup. It was forged

LAMINATED VASE, 32 INCHES HIGH.

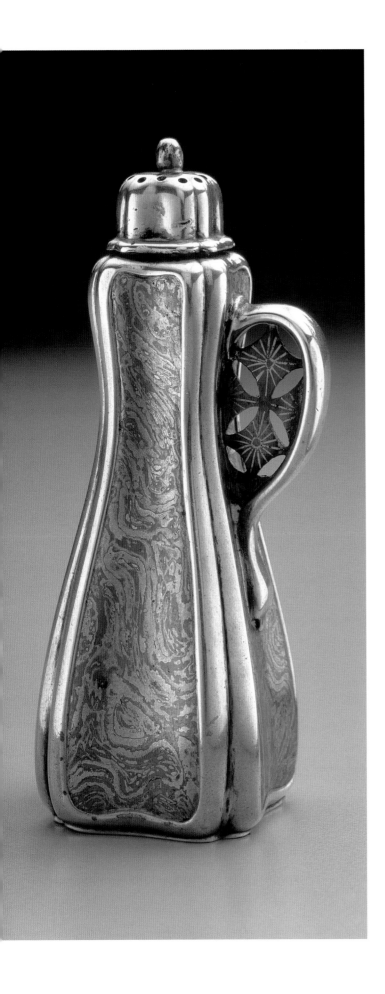

LEFT:

✍ *Mokume* sugar caster designed by
Edward C. Moore circa 1879. ✍

ABOVE:

✍ *Mokume* tea caddy, 4½ inches tall,
designed by Edward C. Moore and made
in 1880. The ivory finial is a *netsuke* that
was probably part of the collection
brought from Japan to Tiffany's in 1877
by Christopher Dresser. ✍

OPPOSITE:

⮞ Japanesque jardinière made in 1879, possibly designed by Edward C. Moore with Charles Osborne. The 10¼-inch-tall piece has the traditional *horo* form, and the handles appear to be simplified versions of "fish dragon" handles that appear very rarely on mid-fourteenth-century Chinese porcelain. The lower body is chased as a pond with sprays of reeds and lilies, and has applied green and yellow-gold flowers and leaves decorated with copper. Four copper-and-brass turtles on the shoulder crawl towards the rim, a fifth turtle pokes his head above the water near the base, and one of the handles has a partly gilt copper bug. Moore based the turtles on a Japanese turtle in his own collection: it is now at the Metropolitan Museum of Art. The jardinière sold at Sotheby's for $159,500 on June 27, 1990. ⮜

⮞ Archival photograph showing a pair of Japanesque vases decorated with dancing frogs and the initials "AA" surmounted by Russian imperial crowns. The snail-like repoussé forms above the base are characteristic of Charles Osborne's work, indicating that the vases were made after Osborne joined Tiffany's in January 1879. They were made for the Grand Duke Alexis Alexandrovitch, who appears just below the Prince of Wales at the head of the "List of Purchasers" published by Tiffany's at the close of the 1878 Paris Exposition. The vases may have been Tiffany's present to him, like the loving cup Tiffany's presented to the Prince of Wales in 1883 (see page 101). Grand Duke Alexis was the third son of Czar Alexander II, a brother of Alexander III, and an uncle of Nicholas II. Born in 1850, he spent his entire career in the Russian navy, which he commanded as High Admiral from 1881 until 1904. In the fall and winter of 1871–72, Alexis came to the United States on the cruiser *Svetlana*, and during his tour of the country he went buffalo hunting with William F. ("Buffalo Bill") Cody. Cody later recalled, "The Grand Duke was the finest foreign gentleman I ever conducted on a hunt. He sat on his horse like a—well, like me. He shot—well, like me. He was the strongest man I have ever seen. Once he lifted a broncho [sic], saddle and all. He made friends with the Indians and they followed him about like a shadow." (*The New York Times*, November 15, 1908) ⮜

LEFT:

This Japanesque tray, 11 inches in diameter, has inlays of platinum and various shades of copper and gold depicting three butterflies: a swallowtail and two tropical *Nymphalidae*. Designed by Edward C. Moore circa 1880, it may have been an homage to James Abbott McNeill Whistler (1834–1903), the brilliant American artist who championed Japanese art and used a butterfly as his signature. Several versions of this tray are known; one sold for $23,000 at Sotheby's on January 20, 1998.

BELOW:

Archival photograph taken in 1878 showing a Japanesque tray with butterflies and a dragonfly, and a gourd-shaped vase with spiral chasing. Identical butterflies were used on the tray illustrated above.

Emaneling pattern for menu card holders for the Mackay silver service, which was shown at the 1878 Paris Exposition. The card holders were an addition designed by Moore and made in 1880.

ENAMELING DESIGN FOR BUTTERFLY–CARD– –RACK No 0359

No 03

280

BELOW:

Japanesque double tea caddy, circa 1880, shaped as a butterfly whose coloring is depicted in patinated copper and yellow metal. The hinged wings form the lids of two compartments with gilt interiors.

Engraved 12-inch-tall teakettle and burner designed by Edward C. Moore about 1879; it originally had a matching sugar bowl and creamer. Charles L. Venable, curator of decorative arts at the Dallas Museum of Art, wrote of this piece: "Here not only the figures and plant forms are probably derived from a work like [Katsushika Hokusai's sketchbook] *Manga*, but the vessel's shape is Asian. The Y-shaped legs are reminiscent of supports found on Ming dynasty Chinese furniture, and the pot's form is close to Japanese porcelain examples fitted with bamboo or reed handles of similar squared profile." (*Silver in America*, 1994) Christopher Dresser designed a traveling tea set with a pot of almost identical shape but with a folding handle.

Five-inch-tall Japanesque teapot with an applied copper butterfly and a gold gourd on a vine. Designed by Edward C. Moore circa 1878.

Japanesque teapot with a boxwood handle and a jade finial designed by Edward C. Moore circa 1885.

A photograph of Tiffany merchandise on display at the Paris Exposition of 1867. The "Moresque" tea set is at the lower right. ✍

✍ Designed by Edward C. Moore for the 1867 Exposition Universelle in Paris, this tea set is one of Moore's early works in the Orientalist vein. He called its style "Moresque" because he based its engraved split-leaf patterns on plates 22 and 23 in the second volume of Owen Jones's *Plans, Elevations, Sections and Details of the Alhambra*, the palace of Moorish kings in Granada. He based the elaborate handles of the creamer and sugar bowl on the handle of an early-sixteenth-century Persian brass jug. Jones's book and the Persian jug were in Moore's own collection, which he bequeathed to the Metropolitan Museum of Art. Tiffany's silverware won a bronze medal at the 1867 Paris Exposition, and its advertisements proudly announced that it was "the only award ever made by a foreign country to American manufacturers of silverware." ✍

WIRE WORK FOR ENAMEL
PEPPER No 3147

ABOVE:

Cloisonné enameling patterns dated August 12, 1875, for pepper shakers designed by Edward C. Moore, possibly for the 1876 Philadelphia Exhibition.

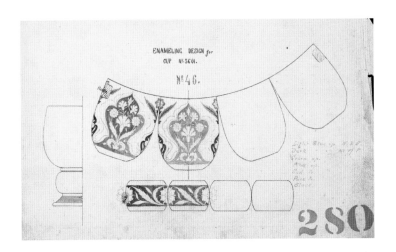

ENAMELING DESIGN for
CUP No 5601.
No 46.

ABOVE:

Enameling patterns for Edward C. Moore designs, possibly drawn by Moore and colored by his assistants. They appear to be for a silver footed cup to be shown at the 1876 Philadelphia Exhibition.

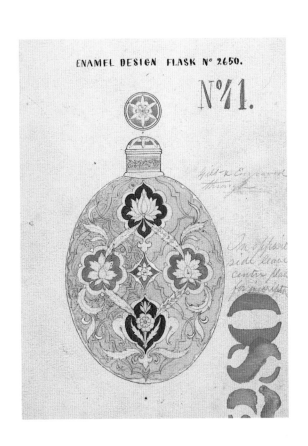

ENAMEL DESIGN FLASK No 2650.
No 1.

LEFT:

"Persian" enameling pattern for a flask designed by Edward C. Moore, possibly drawn by him and colored by Tiffany's design studio. This pattern is dated February 8, 1876.

LEFT:

This 8-inch-tall pitcher has a quatrefoil cross section and alternating bands of silver decorated with flowers and bands of copper inlaid with silver patterns. Tiffany & Co. showed it at the 1876 Philadelphia Centennial Exhibition as part of a "Group of Silver Articles, chromatically decorated by inlaying with copper, gold, and niello enamel—the first examples produced here." Tiffany's was boasting that these were the first inlaid-silver pieces made in America; since a law prohibited British silversmiths from "adulterating" their wares with other materials, Tiffany's led the world in "mixed-metal" hollowware until it went out of fashion in the early years of the twentieth century. This pitcher was purchased at the exhibition by Gideon F. T. Reed for the Museum of Fine Arts in Boston; it was the first Tiffany piece acquired by a museum and the first work of American silver to enter that museum's collection. Reed, a Bostonian and a major shareholder in Tiffany & Co., had opened the company's Paris branch in 1850.

OPPOSITE:

Tiffany & Co. vice president Charles T. Cook commissioned this coffeepot designed by Edward C. Moore in 1874 and lent it to Tiffany's for its display at the 1876 Centennial Exhibition in Philadelphia. *Harper's Weekly* praised it highly, describing it as "a delicate and graceful coffee-pot of Persian design, which is covered with a profusion of flowers and leaves, after the lavish manner of the East, and while it is one of the simplest objects among those we illustrate, still [it] possesses a general symmetry and truthfulness of outline unsurpassed by any other in the collection." (November 4, 1876, p. 890) Moore based its form and floral decoration—organized by long serrated leaves called "saz" that are characteristic of Ottoman art—on ceramic water bottles made in Iznik in the sixteenth century; although Iznik is in Turkey, its style was strongly influenced by Persia.

Probably designed by Edward C. Moore in 1888, the form and decoration of this Saracenic enameled and parcel-gilt tea set is similar to the Macy Cup (see page 70) shown at the 1889 Paris Exposition. It was purchased by Cornelia Ann Atwill, who later purchased the Magnolia Vase and Daisy Vase at the 1893 Chicago Exposition (see pages 185 and 190). The bottoms of the teapot, creamer, and sugar bowl are engraved with a large monogram, "CAA." When Mrs. Atwill gave the set to the Metropolitan Museum of Art in 1897, Tiffany's wrote a letter saying that it was made "entirely by hand . . . without seams . . . each . . . from a single piece of silver. It is enameled, etched and gilded; and is also etched and gilded on the interior, which in itself is a very difficult and remarkable piece of work." (Quoted in *Nineteenth Century America*, 1970)

Edward C. Moore and John T. Curran's original drawings for the covered sugar bowl above.

OPPOSITE:

Brightly-colored Saracenic tea caddy designed by Edward C. Moore and made on February 18, 1889. Its enameling patterns were by John T. Curran, and its etching and enameling cost was $145. Another version with a carved ivory top had an etching and enameling cost of $360.

OPPOSITE:

↗ Etched and enameled
Orientalist teapot with a
crescent-moon ivory finial,
designed by Edward C.
Moore circa 1889. ↘

↗ This 4¾-inch-tall pepper mill is decorated with pale yellow, pale blue, white,
ochre, lavender, and bright-red champlevé shaded enamel. It appears to have been
designed by John T. Curran circa 1890: its swirling forms—inspired by the work of
Charles Osborne—are similar to Curran's Tarpon and Seaweed Vases shown at the 1893
Chicago Exposition (see page 189). Inscribed on the base "L.C.T. from E.C.M.," it was
given to Louis Comfort Tiffany by Edward C. Moore; they shared an interest in Orientalism,
and Moore may have thought Louis Tiffany would appreciate its proto-Art Nouveau design.
It sold for $37,375 on January 20, 1998, at Sotheby's. Tiffany's showed similar pepper mills
with red and black enamel pepper seeds at the Chicago Exposition; André Bouilhet called
them "truly jewels which one would be pleased to use. This, to my idea, is true luxury,
and it must be one of the greatest enjoyments of wealth to be able to be surrounded by
objects for daily use, the artistic character of which enhances the joy of possession." (*The
Jewelers' Review*, October 16, 1893) ↘

are in imitation of the shoots of broad leaved, fleshy plants. The floral subjects are small, perhaps Easter flowers or heliotrope. The base is shaped like a kettle, while about two-thirds of the body are conical in form, terminating in a hemispherical lid, which is surmounted by an ornamental knob.

The elephant's foot loving cup is a unique piece which cannot fail to command attention. Its name is derived from its form, which is that of the fore foot of an Asiatic elephant. It is engraved and

bowl and cream pitcher. Each piece is ornamented with mountings and repoussé bosses in which are set large, rough pearls, such as are termed *barocque*. This combination of silver and pearls is exceedingly artistic and quite novel, having, we are informed, not been attempted by other silversmiths. The set is decidedly rich, dainty and refined. The price of this elegant service is $1,200.

A hand mirror and puff box are finished in a style similar to the tête-à-tête set just described. Both

ELEPHANT'S FOOT LOVING CUP.

inlaid with niello in graceful, curved lines. Figures representing two ostriches appear on its front. The handles are excellent representations of elephants' tusks, united to the bowl at the top by figures of palm leaves mingled with graceful scrolls. It is one of our subjects of illustration, and will probably never return to America, as it is a tempting piece of ornamental silver.

A small tête-à-tête set which is generally admired consists of three pieces. They are a teapot, sugar

are richly embossed and set with large pearls. They are worthy a place on the toilet table of any lady. The price of the two pieces is $1,000.

A novel and handsome style of decoration is shown in a coffee pot of slender form, ornamented with butterflies which appear to have just alighted upon it. The bodies of the beautiful moths are of parcel gilt and their wings are inlaid with selected pieces of pearl shell of most brilliant coloring, appearing in changing lights almost as handsome as opals. The

LEFT:

❧ Designed by Edward C. Moore, this Indian-style "Elephant's Foot" loving cup was made for the 1889 Paris Exposition (see photograph on page 2). *The Jewelers' Weekly* called it "a unique piece that cannot fail to command attention. Its name is derived from its form, which is that of the fore foot of an Asiatic elephant. It is engraved and inlaid with niello in graceful, curved lines. Figures representing two ostriches [actually peacocks] appear on its front. The handles are excellent representations of elephant's tusks, united to the bowl at the top by figures of palm leaves mingled with graceful scrolls. It . . . will probably never return to America, as it is a tempting piece of ornamental silver." (May 30, 1889) (see the recent color photo on page 2). ❧

ABOVE:

❧ Edward C. Moore and John T. Curran's enameling pattern for the two peacocks, dated February 16, 1889. ❧

OPPOSITE:

❧ Another version of the same cup with stylized flowers rather than peacocks. ❧

↗ Probably designed by Edward C. Moore with the collaboration of John T. Curran, this enameled loving cup was shown at the 1889 Paris Exposition. *The Jewelers' Weekly* reported, that this "loving cup of exceptional beauty is 9½ inches high and 9 inches in diameter. It is strictly 'Saracenic' in form and decoration. It seems to grow from a richly carved rosette beneath its body into six large swells and becomes round at the top. The decoration consists of large flowers near the bottom, chased and enameled and connected by graceful 'Saracenic' lines with the enameled bosses and flowers at the top of the cup. It was forged from one piece of silver, and there is no seam or solder in it except at the points where the three perforated handles are united." (May 30, 1889) The cup was presented to Valentine Everit Macy (1871–1930) on his twenty-first birthday, March 23, 1892. The heir to a Standard Oil fortune, young Macy was to devote much of his career to public service and philanthropy: he was director of welfare services for New York's Westchester County from 1914 to 1924 and president of the county's Park Commission from 1926 until 1930. In 1917 President Woodrow Wilson appointed him chairman of a commission to resolve shipyard labor disputes, and in 1919 he arbitrated a New York City harbor strike. His donations to the Metropolitan Museum of Art included a number of Islamic pieces, and his aunt, Mrs. William M. (Mary Jane Macy) Kingsland gave the museum an Islamic-style longcase clock dated 1882 made by Tiffany & Co. that may also have been designed by Edward C. Moore. ↘

RIGHT:

↗ Edward C. Moore and John T. Curran's enameling pattern for this cup, dated March 2, 1889. ↘

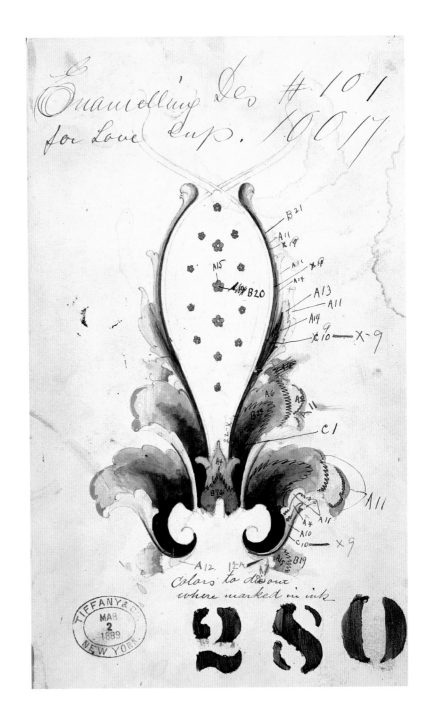

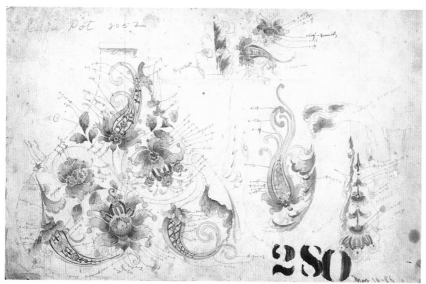

The Saracenic coffeepot in the photograph opposite was designed in 1886 by Edward C. Moore, whose original drawing is at top right. It was made for the 1889 Paris Exposition using John T. Curran's enameling pattern at the lower right. *The Jewelers' Weekly* reported on Tiffany's "objects of Saracenic design" at the Exposition: "Some of them are chased in repoussé with delicate lines of enamel introduced, and in many instances are elaborated with a groundwork of etching." (May 30, 1889) The tray and sweetmeat dish illustrated opposite, designed under Moore's direction, completed this unusual three-piece set. This set sold at Christie's on June 19, 1990 for $44,000. Three more versions of the coffeepot were made in the 1890s, one of which used the enameling pattern at opposite bottom.

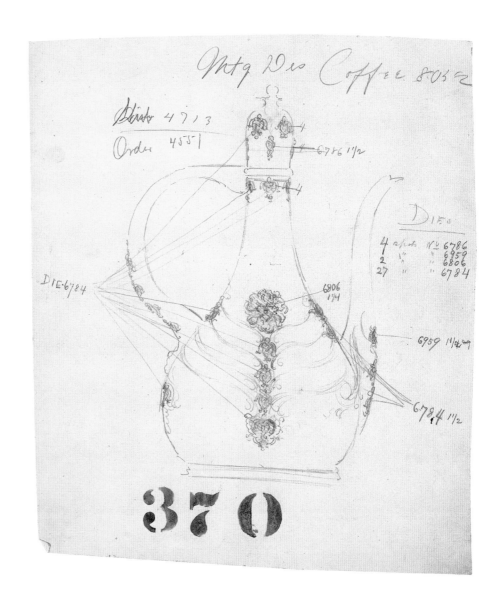

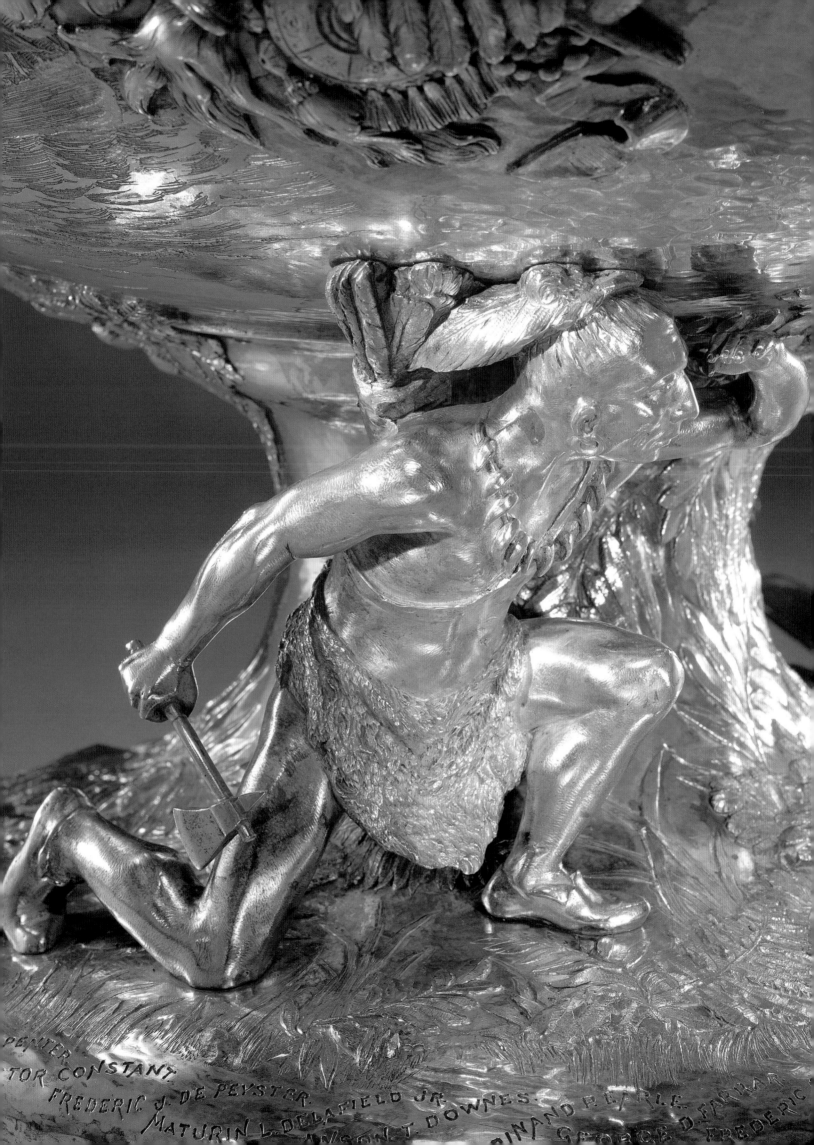

PEYSTER.
TOR CONSTANT.
FREDERIC J. DE PEYSTER.
MATURIN L. DELAFIELD JR.
ANSON J. DOWNES.
DINAND PEARLE.
GEORGE D. FARRAR.
FREDERIC

CHAPTER 2:
AMERICAN VICTORIANISM

JAMES HORTON WHITEHOUSE
EUGENE JULIUS SOLIGNY
CHARLES T. GROSJEAN

✍ Members of the Societies of Colonial Wars are descendants of officers and men who fought in wars in the colonies that became the thirteen original United States, primarily in the 1754 French and Indian War. Forty-three members of the Society of Colonial Wars in the State of New York commissioned this imposing punch bowl initiated on December 19, 1893 at the society's second annual banquet. *The New-York Daily Tribune* illustrated the bowl with this description: "It weighs 298 ounces, stands 13½ inches high, and is 18½ inches in diameter. The story of the Colonial wars is pictured in bas-relief, repoussé, and etched work around the body and base. Two figures are on the base, one representing a North American Indian crouching on one side of the stem, and a Colonial soldier on the other, both in correct historical attire. Around the body of the bowl are arranged the shields of the original colonies. A series of Colonial coins are also set at intervals in the surface of the bowl, and a gold coin is set in the ladle." (December 20, 1893) The design is by James H. Whitehouse, and the figures were undoubtedly modeled by Eugene J. Soligny. ✎

J ames Horton Whitehouse was the first important silversmith Edward C. Moore brought to Tiffany & Co. to collaborate on design.

Born on October 28, 1833, in Handsworth, Staffordshire, England, Whitehouse was educated at King Edward's School in Birmingham, England's metalworking center and home of its leading silver manufacturer, Elkington & Co. He immigrated to America at age twenty-two in 1855, the year he first appears in the Brooklyn City Directory as an "engraver" living at 36 Prospect Street and working at 10 Front Street for Henry A. Brown, a manufacturer of diamond-pointed gold pens. (Brown may well have been a supplier of Tiffany & Co.) Whitehouse was hired by Tiffany on May 2, 1858, for his exceptional skills as both designer and engraver. Records do not show whether or not he ever actually worked for Elkington's after completing school and before immigrating to America, but it is a distinct possibility, as George Richards Elkington was a governor of King Edward's School and would have been alert to employing its most talented metalworking students.

In any case, Edward C. Moore recognized Tiffany's American clientele's taste for silver in the neoclassic sculpted and engraved style of Elkington's. Some months earlier that taste had prompted Gorham, Tiffany's principal competitor in the silver trade, to hire another Englishman, Birmingham School of Design–trained George Wilkinson, as its chief designer. In Whitehouse, Moore hoped to employ Wilkinson's equal.

At Tiffany & Co., Whitehouse was immediately commissioned to design a medal to be struck in commemoration of the laying of the first transatlantic cable by Cyrus W. Field in 1858. The Field medal was significant to Charles Lewis Tiffany, who had greatly profited from Field's achievement by buying up miles of leftover cable and reselling it in lengths of four inches or less, which he had made up into a line of commemorative paperweights, watch fobs, cane handles, and seals.

In 1860 one of Whitehouse's younger brothers, Frederick (1835–1880), also an engraver, came to New York where he lived in the household of his brother from 1860 to 1866. During these times he worked for William Bogert & Co., which produced ornate silver in an Americanized Elkington style exclusively for Tiffany & Co. from 1866 to 1869, and where Charles T. Grosjean also worked.

Probably the first of many horse-racing trophies designed by James H. Whitehouse and Eugene J. Soligny, the 34-inch-tall Woodlawn Vase is the most fabled trophy in American horse-racing history. The trophy was commissioned in 1860 by R. Aitcheson Alexander, born in Frankfort, Kentucky, in 1810. In 1823 he went to England to be educated under the aegis of his bachelor uncle, Sir William Alexander, whose fortune he inherited. He returned to Kentucky in 1851 or 1852 after having taken over his father's Woodburn Farm, which he turned into the largest stud farm in the world. Woodburn Farm's Lexington sired 231 winners: the best known was Milton H. Sanford's Preakness, for whom the Preakness Stakes is named. Alexander commissioned this trophy for an unusual competition at the Woodlawn Race Course near Louisville: if one owner's horse won races for the cup at three successive meetings at Woodlawn, he would win the cup, but then it was subject to challenge from other owners. The first race, on May 18, 1861, was won by Thomas G. Moore's Mollie Jackson, and Moore's Idlewild won the following year, putting Moore two legs up. But raids during the Civil War obliged Alexander to send his breeding stock to Canada and bury the great vase at Woodburn. Its history over the next few years is obscure, but one of Alexander's horses evidently won the 1867 race at Woodlawn. Alexander died that year, and Woodlawn ceased operations in 1870. Eight years later the trophy was won by Mike and Phil Dwyer's Bramble in the American Stallion Stakes at Churchill Downs. The Dwyers took it to New York, and during the next twenty-six years it was raced for at Coney Island, Jerome Park, and Morris Park. Thomas C. Clyde's Shorthose won it at Morris Park in 1903 and again in 1904. Clyde held the vase for several years, then gave it to the

Maryland Jockey Club, operator of the Pimlico Racetrack, and it was first offered in 1917 as a "perpetual" trophy for the Preakness Stakes. ("Perpetuals" must be handed over to winners of subsequent races.) The trophy does not survive in its original form. Over the years several of the original figures—the jockey on the topmost horse, the angels, and the horses and elephant on the base—disappeared, and some were replaced with inferior copies. After Alfred G. Vanderbilt's Native Dancer won the Preakness in 1953, his wife persuaded Vanderbilt to donate it to the Maryland Jockey Club to save it from further destruction. Since then Preakness winners have been given 21-inch-tall replicas; the original is kept at the Maryland Historical Society and brought to Pimlico for the annual running of the Preakness.

During the Civil War, James Whitehouse devoted his talents to numerous medals, presentation swords, and other testimonials presented to assorted heroes of the war. He also designed the corps badges used by the Union Army. At the end of the war in 1865, Whitehouse encouraged two of his younger brothers (or possibly one brother and one cousin) to come to New York. Joseph Charles Whitehouse (1838–1895) arrived in 1866 and was employed by Tiffany & Co. as a watchmaker, an employment he retained for the rest of his life. Edward Whitehouse arrived a year after Joseph, beginning as an engraver in 1867.

It is interesting to note that two of James Horton Whitehouse's sons were both undoubtedly trained in Edward C. Moore's Tiffany School and would both later work for Tiffany & Co. as well. The elder son, James Whitehouse Jr., (1858–1929) began at Tiffany's as a jeweler in 1879; the second son, Frederick W. Whitehouse (1865–1929) began in 1887 as an artist-designer like his father.

✐ Designed by James H. Whitehouse, this silver, iron, and gold sword and scabbard were presented in 1864 to General John Wynn Davidson, the hero of Bayou Meto and Little Rock, by privates and noncommissioned officers of the First Iowa Veteran Cavalry. The hilt includes a personification of Liberty topped with an American eagle, and the scabbard has General Davidson's monogram. This was one of hundreds of swords that Tiffany's made for presentation to Union officers during the Civil War. ✐

The completion of the laying of the first transatlantic telegraph cable in August 1858 was widely celebrated by New Yorkers, in part because what we now call the "global information age" had just begun, but mostly because it had been accomplished by a New York company. On September 1 the city held a Cable Jubilee at the Crystal Palace on Reservoir Square (now Bryant Park) at Sixth Avenue and Forty-second Street, where Mayor Fernando Wood presented Cyrus W. Field—the cable company's founder, head, and driving force—with this 4½-by-2¾-inch gold box engraved by James H. Whitehouse. The scene on the cover shows two cable-laying ships—*Niagara* and *Agamemnon*—when the cable had just been spliced in the middle of the Atlantic and the two ships were paying out the cable over their sterns. The scene on the left end of the box shows the first meeting of the cable company's investors in Field's house, and the scene on the right end shows the landing of the cable at Trinity Bay in Newfoundland. The excitement aroused by the cable's completion dissipated when it failed after only three weeks of service, but Field persisted and his company completed the first permanent transatlantic cable in 1866.

All that considered, by the time of the Paris 1867 Exposition Tiffany & Co. had three Birmingham-trained craftsmen/designers from the Whitehouse family. While James, foreman of the silver shop under Edward C. Moore, was clearly in charge, any of them could well have been responsible for the affinities to Birmingham's style that Tiffany silver showed at the Paris Exposition of 1867.

Edward C. Moore's enlightened and superior design direction and extraordinary craftsmanship had encouraged the Whitehouses' talents to exceed their Birmingham origins to the point that Elkington's itself asked to buy the entire award-winning Tiffany exhibit as prototypes; refused, the firm contented itself with a smaller selection of the display wares.

That same year, James Whitehouse designed his first surviving major work of presentation silver, the "Westchester Cup for the Summer Races at Jerome Park" in the Bronx at the site currently occupied by the Jerome Park reservoir. The Jerome Park Cup is typical of Whitehouse's work, which was most often severe in form and elaborate in detail. As well as an engraver and designer, Whitehouse was also a stone cutter, and his style could be labeled "lapidary"—minutely detailed but sometimes wanting in the overall harmony of its parts.

The iconography of the "Jerome Park Cup—Sleepy Hollow" trophy, as it is listed in Tiffany's ledgers, includes two racehorses ridden by their jockeys, the Halloween woodland chase of Ichabod Crane and the Headless Horseman (to call to mind Washington Irving's "The Legend of Sleepy Hollow"), and finally a feather-headressed Indian standing proudly atop the 27½-inch-high, 265-ounce monument to the early days of Westchester County and New York horseracing. Whitehouse did his best to unite the unlikely cast through a three-storied architecture of his habitual neoclassic severity; however, this trophy offers more eclectic period charm than aesthetic harmony.

It was first displayed at Tiffany & Co.'s 550 Broadway store in late May 1867 before the Westchester Cup race run on Thursday, June 20, 1867. The *New York Times*, which was partial to Jerome Park—the park's owner, Leonard Jerome, having been for many years the *Times's* principal owner—described it eloquently on May 21:

> It is a very chaste and valuable specimen of workmanship and courts the admiration of many visitors. It is of silver, stands 28 inches high, weighs 300 ounces, and is valued at $3,000. The base, burnished and oxidized, represents the track, on which are delicately wrought the leaves and grass indented by the hoofs of the horses. From the centre of this circular track rises the pedestal, burnished and embraced by a band of posted silver bearing the inscription "Jerome Park." From the pedestal rise four slender pillars, surmounted by a dome, upon the top of which is the stalwart figure of an Indian, war-painted, and feathered resting on his bow. Under the dome, the central point of observation, is represented with great fidelity that fearful moment in the legend of Sleepy Hollow, when Ichabod, followed by the headless ghost, plunges headlong down the hill on his no less affrighted *Gunpowder*. The fear which fills both terrified horse and master is admirable given in the expressive faces of both; while the motionless metal seems to move, so successfully are the lines denoting excited action given. The headless goblin (nursing the pumpkin on the pommel of his saddle) follows fast behind; both horse and rider showing all the eagerness of the chase. Underneath this central group and on the track around the pedestal before described, are the figures of two racers and their riders "walking the course."

Archival photograph of a cigar box, probably designed by James H. Whitehouse with modeling and chasing by Eugene J. Soligny. James Gordon Bennett commissioned the box circa 1876; Tiffany's ledger reads, "Segar Box 'Horse' (Bennett) Each 625.00." The present whereabouts of this remarkable object is unknown.

A rook from the silver and gold chess set with an ebony and mother-of pearl chessboard presented by the New York Chess Club to Paul Morphy, "the chess champion of the world," in a ceremony at the New York University assembly hall on May 25, 1859. Probably designed by James H. Whitehouse, the chess set was not custom made: in January 1858 Tiffany's had displayed it in the window of its store at 550 Broadway with a price of $1,500, but when the Chess Club decided to present it to Morphy, Tiffany's sold it to them at cost. Morphy was born in New Orleans in 1837. When he was in his early teens, he won forty-five out of fifty matches with America's leading master, Eugene Rousseau. He arrived in New York on October 5, 1857, for the first Congress of the American Chess Association. *Frank Leslie's Illustrated Newspaper* commented, "Notwithstanding his high reputation, there were many, who, from his youth and the small number of his published games, manifested much incredulity concerning his chess strength. But on the evening of his arrival all doubts were removed in the minds of those who witnessed his passages at arms with Mr. Stanley . . . and the first prize was universally conceded him, even before the entries . . . had been completed." (June 4, 1859) In 1858 he traveled to Europe, winning matches by overwhelming scores against nearly all prominent masters, including Adolf Anderssen, who had won the first international chess tournament held in London in 1857. Not long after the presentation at University Hall, Morphy retired and never played chess again. After his death in New Orleans in 1884, his chess set was sold at auction to Walter Denegre, but its subsequent history is murky: many have attempted to find it, all to no avail. Contemporary masters who have studied Morphy's published games consider him the greatest chess player of all time.

One of the horses is a portrait of the famous *Gladiateur*, the other an American horse, unnamed. [The other horse is *Kentucky*.] The design, in its completeness, represents three stages of civilization in Westchester County—the days of the Aborigines, the legendary time of Sleepy Hollow, and the present day, when wealth and fashion court for pleasure the scene once the solitary domain of the native hunter, and later that wherein the poet tale-teller conjures up the immemorable figures of Ichabod and Rip Van Winkle.

His next surviving work of presentation silver, a monumental centerpiece commemorating the inauguration in July 1871 of Peru's Mollendo-Arequipa Railway built by "Yankee Pizarro" Henry Meiggs, although unsigned, is stylistically so perfectly in keeping with his work as to be legitimately attributed to him.

This design is, again, at once an elaborate and severe neoclassic architecture (this time standing 41½ inches high and weighing a whopping 784 ounces). Its Empire Revival quatrefoil base is incongruously guarded by four poncho-clad native Peruvian laborers; its summit is crowned by an allegorical figure of America; and in between, issuing from acanthus whorls, four putti terms support an octagonal central standard ornamented with bows and arrows, fascia, and four spiraling cornucopias spilling out tropical fruits. The Chilean newspaper *El Mercurio* described it on July 28, 1871, as "worked with such exquisite taste and attention to detail that it seems more a jewelers' work." The writer's description could well stand for all of Whitehouse's silver designs.

Shortly after the Meiggs centerpiece, Whitehouse began work on designs for the William Cullen Bryant silver vase to commemorate the doyen of American poets' eightieth birthday, November 3, 1874. The vase was completed in time for the Philadelphia Centennial Exposition of 1876, where it was put on public display and generally acclaimed as the greatest work in *repoussé* chased silver yet made in America. An article in *Harpers New Monthly Magazine* (July 1876) accurately described the Whitehouse style "in its severity of form and in its careful and exquisite details." In that same article, James Whitehouse went on record commenting on his work: "When the Bryant testimonial was first mentioned to me, my thoughts at once flew to the country—to the crossing of the boughs of trees, to the plants and flowers, and to a general contemplation of Nature; and these, together with a certain Homeric influence,

Eugene Soligny's sketch for the Indian warrior atop the Jerome Park Trophy.

The Jerome Park racetrack was built in 1865 by Leonard W. Jerome (Winston Churchill's grandfather) just north of Manhattan in what was then Westchester County; the site is now occupied by the Jerome Park Reservoir in the Bronx. The racetrack was a great success, and New Yorkers lined Fifth Avenue to watch nearly continuous parades of carriages taking the "swells" up to the races. The Westchester Cup, awarded at Jerome Park on June 20, 1867, was designed by James H. Whitehouse and modeled and chased by Eugene J. Soligny. *Wilkes' Spirit of the Times, A Chronicle of the Turf, Field Sports, and the Stage* commented: "This was a fine piece of plate of the value of $1,500 in specie [Tiffany's ledger lists the manufacturing cost at $3,624, so the actual value was a whopping $7,000]. . . . The design of the Cup, which was exhibited in front of the grand stand, is very good. At the base there are statuettes of two race-horses [Gladiateur and Kentucky, the most famous English and American racehorses of the time] with their jockeys up. On the cover there are two other statuettes, representing the headless horseman of Sleepy Hollow in pursuit of Ichabod Crane, or whoever it was that came across the mounted spectre. An arch like that at the entrance to the Club grounds stretches over these latter-mentioned figures, and this is rather an anomaly, for it is not to be supposed that there were any arches in Sleepy Hollow except those formed by the twisted trunks and limbs of forest trees. The whole is surmounted by a statuette of an Indian hunter with an unstrung bow. As we said before, the design is good, but the figures of the race-horses are not at all well executed. Gladiateur's forelegs remind us of the legs of a saw-buck, and he has besides a capped hock, and a long tail, not squared. On the other side Kentucky is calf-kneed, and not a bit like the hero of the two Saratoga Cups and the Inauguration Stake." There were four horses in the race for the Westchester Cup, and the winner was Milton H. Sanford's Loadstone. (*Wilkes' Spirit*, June 22, 1867) Three years later, on the October 25, 1870, opening day of the Pimlico Race Track, Milton Sanford's colt Preakness won the Dinner Party Stakes; the Preakness Stakes, one of the races in the "triple crown," was named for Sanford's three-year-old.

produced in my mind the germ of the design—the form of a Greek vase, with the most beautiful American flowers growing round and entwining themselves gracefully about it, each breathing its own particular story as it grew."

The Bryant Vase (on display at the Metropolitan Museum of Art, to whom Bryant donated it in 1877) is without doubt to this day the most remarkable American work in hand-chased repoussé silver and the masterpiece of the Whitehouse style. Tiffany's was so proud of it that four electroformed copies were made, and one was sent to the Paris Exposition of 1878, where it won high praise.

The Bryant Vase completed, Whitehouse immediately began assisting Edward C. Moore in preparing other designs for the Paris Exposition of 1878. Most notably, he would focus on the exquisite detailing of the ornamental motifs on Moore's spectacular 1,250-piece dinner-and-dessert service made for "Silver Bonanza King" John Mackay from 14,719 ounces of silver Mackay had shipped directly to Tiffany & Co. in 1877 from his Comstock Lode mine.

The shapes of the Mackay service, however, are credited to Charles Grosjean and are an interpretation of Edward C. Moore's graceful and volumetric, organic forms, not of Whitehouse's severe neoclassic vocabulary of architectural ornament; but the ornament of the Mackay service, although sometimes also credited to Grosjean, was clearly under Moore's direction with its combined Islamic and occasional Japanesque details. In many of its ordered patternings and in its exquisite repoussé detailing it suggests Whitehouse's participation as well. In any case, the Mackay service took about two hundred silversmiths nearly two years to complete, requiring forty chasers alone. It is doubtful that there was a single man at Tiffany's Prince Street works who did not participate in its production.

The frenzy of the Mackay service over in 1878, Whitehouse began work on an elaborately jeweled and enameled neo-Gothic silver casket to be presented to Episcopal bishop of New York Horatio Potter on the twenty-fifth anniversary of his entering the ministry, November 25, 1879. (It was not completed until April, 1880.) Now in the collection of New York's Cathedral of St. John the Divine, this extraordinary object was described in a biographical sketch published during Whitehouse's lifetime as "wrought by the repoussé process, the golden enrichments are carved by hand, and the

Parcel-gilt presentation vase with sculptured putti spearing dragons. The inscription reads, "Thirty six members of the Union League Club unite in presenting this vase to Thomas Nast as a token of their admiration of his genius and of his ardent devotion of that genius to the preservation of his country from the schemes of rebellion[,] April 1869." The Union League Club was founded on February 24, 1863, by members of the Union Club who were outraged by that club's declining to expel a Southerner who expressed sympathy with the Confederacy. Thomas Nast (1840–1902) first gained fame for his anti-Confederate cartoons in *Harper's Weekly*. After the war ended in 1865, the Union League Club became the chief bastion of Republican Party strength in New York City. Four months before this vase was presented, allies of the Democratic Party's Tammany Hall faction had taken office as governor of New York State and mayor of New York City. Republicans counterattacked with accusations of corruption on the part of Tammany boss William M. Tweed, and it's likely that the thirty-six members of the Union League Club intended this vase to enlist Nast's support in their cause. If so, they certainly succeeded, for Nast's famous caricatures of Tweed have been credited with causing his downfall in 1871. Nast's widow gave the vase to the Metropolitan Museum of Art in 1907.

THIRTY SIX MEMBERS
OF THE
Union League Club
UNITE IN PRESENTING THIS VASE
TO
Thomas Nast
AS A TOKEN OF THEIR ADMIRATION
of his genius and of his ardent devotion
of that genius to the preservation of his
country from the schemes of rebellion
APRIL 1869.

✐ Like the Bartholdi Testimonial (see page 99), the Gladstone Testimonial was a promotion by Joseph Pulitzer's newspaper *The World*. Many of its readers were Irish-Americans, and on July 23, 1886, Pulitzer called on its readers to contribute to a testimonial to British Prime Minister William E. Gladstone in gratitude for his sponsoring a bill giving Home Rule to Ireland. *The World* itself contributed $100 and asked its readers to contribute 25 cents each "to make the Testimonial representative of a great many people of all classes." The defeat of the Home Rule bill in the fall of 1886 brought down Gladstone's Liberal government, adding to the public's admiration for his courage: 10,689 contributors eventually sent in a total of $3,382.09, an average of 32 cents each. The 37-inch-tall trophy was completed in May 1887, when it was displayed at Tiffany's store. Surmounted by a bust of Gladstone, it features a female figure with a harp gazing up at the bust; as *The World* put it, "It is as if the symbolized daughter of Ireland in America had paused by the pedestal of the bust to pay merited homage to the Grand Old Man, who is fighting so valiantly for the welfare of her kindred." The axes on the base refer to Gladstone's favorite form of exercise, felling trees on his estate. The photograph below shows Pulitzer (at left with his wife) at the presentation ceremony with Gladstone (at right with his wife) at Gladstone's house outside London on July 9. ✐

OPPOSITE:

✐ In 1866, at the age of twenty-five, James Gordon Bennett, Jr. became managing editor of his father's newspaper, *The New York Herald*; in December of that year he won the first transatlantic yacht race—and international admiration for his courage—by skippering his *Henrietta* through a terrible storm in which six crewmen on a competing yacht were lost at sea. Upon his father's retirement in 1867, Bennett took over the *Herald* and founded the *Evening Telegram*, the first newspaper to appeal to the mass public. When he was elected commodore of the New York Yacht Club in 1871, he established three challenge cups to encourage competition. (Most trophies become the absolute property of their winners, but the ownership of challenge cups is provisional: other yachts can win them by challenging them to subsequent races.) The cup illustrated here is the Ocean Challenge Cup, which Bennett established for a round-trip race between the Sandy Hook Lightship off New York harbor and the Brenton Reef Lightship off Newport. Designed by James H. Whitehouse and modeled and chased by Eugene J. Soligny, it is surmounted by a figure of Columbus pointing to a globe, and the body has Viking-prow handles and a scene from Henry Wadsworth Longfellow's poem, "The Wreck of the *Hesperus.*" When it was exhibited at Tiffany's store in August 1871, *The New York Times* called it "a work of art in the precious metals which . . . far surpasses anything of the kind ever produced in this country and fully equals the most elaborate models of plate ornamentation in the Old World." (August 4, 1871) The first race, held in 1872, was won by the schooner *Rambler*, owned by J. Malcolm Forbes, scion of the richest family in Boston. In 1885 Sir Richard Sutton, Bart. brought the *Genesta* across the Atlantic to challenge three important cups: she failed to win the America's Cup, but she sailed home with both the Ocean and the Cape May Challenge Cups. (Bennett had also established the Cape May cup; see page 90.) In accordance with the fifth paragraphs of Bennett's Deeds of Cup, when the cups were "held by foreign yachts," races were to be sailed between the Isle of Wight and Cherbourg. In 1893 R. Phelps Carroll took the *Navahoe* across the Atlantic to challenge both cups, and for various reasons the Royal Yacht Squadron determined that the Prince of Wales's *Britannia* would defend them. The finish of the 120-mile Ocean Challenge Cup race between the *Navahoe* and the *Britannia* occurred after nightfall on September 14; the yachts were seconds apart at the finish line, and the race committee decided that the *Britannia* had come in first. After Carroll protested on the grounds that the finish line was not straight, the committee reversed its decision; its reversal was roundly hailed as "sporting." Subsequent Ocean Challenge Cup races were sailed between New York and Newport, the last in 1934. ✐

Trophy awarded to James Stillman's 122-foot-long *Wanderer*, winner of a $500 subscription race for keel schooners in the New York Yacht Club's June 16, 1875, regatta. Surmounted by a female figure with two horses made from the same casting used for the Commodore's Challenge Cup for Schooners on page 115, it also has sailors made from the castings used for the Cape May Challenge Cup on page 90. When Stillman won this trophy, he was a successful twenty-five-year-old cotton broker and railroad investor. In the early 1880s he became a close friend and business associate of William Rockefeller, John D. Rockefeller's brother and partner in Standard Oil: Stillman's two daughters married William Rockefeller's sons. In 1891 Stillman was elected president of the National City Bank (predecessor of the present-day Citigroup); his ultra-conservative reserve policies greatly strengthened the bank during the Panic of 1893, attracting increases in deposits that made it the largest bank in New York. The trophy is now at Stillman's grandson's estate, Wethersfield Farm in Amenia, New York; the estate is open to the public in the summer.

damaskening was richer and costlier than any similar work produced in this country."

Four years later, in 1884, Whitehouse produced probably his best-known design, the obverse of the Great Seal of the United States, with its arrows and olive branch-brandishing American eagle, a design known to all through its prominence today on the dollar bill. Once Whitehouse's drawings were approved, the Department of State issued the final order for the new Great Seal dies in the form of a letter to Tiffany & Co. from Secretary of State Frederick T. Frelinghuysen dated January 11, 1884.

Also notable amongst the many commemorative works in silver Whitehouse designed during his forty-three years at Tiffany & Co. are the Bartholdi Testimonial presented to Frédéric Auguste Bartholdi, sculptor of the Statue of Liberty, at the event organized by *The World* newspaper publisher Joseph Pulitzer and held November 13, 1886, some two weeks after the inauguration of the statue; and the Transportation Vase made for the World's Columbian Exposition held in Chicago in 1893. Both typify Whitehouse's mix of severe architectural form and often eccentric detail. The Bartholdi Testimonial combines a silver globe resting on a truncated pyramid of petrified wood from Arizona's Petrified Forest surmounted by a replica in silver of the right hand of the Statue of Liberty bearing its familiar torch. The Transportation Vase is a neoclassic urn with a model of protomodernist Chicago architect Louis Sullivan's astonishing entrance to the Transportation Building at the 1893 World's Fair perched precariously on one side of the vase.

On May 2, 1898, Whitehouse was presented a silver loving cup filled with forty American Beauty roses from his associates at Tiffany & Co., marking his fortieth anniversary with the firm. Whitehouse continued designing medals and presentation silver until shortly before his death at his home, 430 Lafayette Avenue, Brooklyn, November 29, 1902, at the age of sixty-nine.

During his career with Tiffany & Co., the *National Cyclopedia of American Biography* pointed out, "nearly every prominent art-piece in silverware and otherwise, produced by Tiffany & Co., has been conceived by Mr. Whitehouse. On account of his extensive studies and research, as well as his rare taste, Mr. Whitehouse is considered an eminent authority on art matters in general, and in the mysteries of heraldry he is probably more deeply versed than any one else in the country."

In 1872 James Gordon Bennett established the Cape May Challenge Cup to further encourage ocean racing. The trophy, designed by James H. Whitehouse, was one of thirteen yachting trophies commissioned by Bennett that Tiffany's displayed at the 1876 Centennial Exhibition in Philadelphia. The cup was the prize for a round-trip race between New York and Cape May, New Jersey, and was first won by A. B. Stockwell's *Dreadnaught* in 1872. Sir Richard Sutton's *Genesta* won the Cape May Challenge Cup in 1885, and thus races were sailed in the English Channel in 1886, 1889, and 1893. In 1893 the Prince of Wales's *Britannia* had an easy victory in a "drifting match" when she defended the Cape May Cup against the challenge of R. Phelps Carroll's *Navahoe*. Eleven years later, after the Prince of Wales had acceded as King Edward VII, it was determined that the *Britannia* should have returned the cup to the New York Yacht Club when the Prince of Wales sold her in 1897. After a lengthy search, equerries found the cup at Sandringham and the King apologetically returned it. Subsequent races were sailed between New York and Cape May: in 1904 both the Cape May and Ocean Challenge Cups were won by Wilson Marshall's 189-foot-long three-masted schooner, *Atlantic*, which won the Cape May Cup again in 1911. The last Cape May Cup race was sailed in 1939.

The Bryant Vase is among the most celebrated works in silver ever made in the United States, partly due to the public's reverence for its honoree, William Cullen Bryant. He became famous in 1821 with the publication of *Poems*, which included "Thanatopsis" and "To a Waterfowl," his best-known poems to this day. In 1829 he became editor of *The Evening Post*, in which he championed free trade, free speech, workers' rights, and the abolition of slavery. He was one of the few Democrats who left the party to found the antislavery Republican Party in 1857, and he was an ardent supporter of the Union cause during the Civil War. On his eightieth birthday, November 3, 1874, fellow members of the Century Association decided to honor him with a testimonial vase. The competition for the design was won in February 1875 by James H. Whitehouse of Tiffany & Co. Completed fifteen months later, the vase was presented to Bryant at Chickering Hall on June 20, 1876. Bryant's portrait medallion was chased by Eugene J. Soligny, and the smaller medallions were modeled by the sculptor Augustus Saint-Gaudens. The vase was first shown to the general public at the 1876 Philadelphia Exhibition, and one writer expressed the general opinion, "It was justly regarded as one of the most beautiful works in the Exhibition, and received, as it justly deserved, the warm admiration and praise of thousands." (James Dabney McCabe, *The Illustrated History of the Centennial Exhibition*, 1877) However, not all critics were impressed: *The Jewelers' Circular and Horological Review* sniffed, "Tiffany & Co. have scarcely done themselves justice in their *pièce de résistance*, the Bryant Vase. . . . There can be no doubt as to the work in detail. It is of the very finest character and most elaborate in every particular, but its artistic effect as a whole is very poor compared to many other pieces of their work." (Vol. 7) One reporter found the Bryant Vase brouhaha overdone: "The great want of Mr. Bryant's existence has been a vase. You can put a vase to so many uses. As a waste basket it is unexcelled, and as a receptacle for old clothes nothing can equal it. If you want to hide anything, there is that vase. If you want to exhibit something, cover the vase with a board and there's your shelf for the exhibition. It is superior to the wall basket for newspapers and magazines, and as a rag bag it is simply beautiful. In that vase you can hide your pocketbook at night, and so circumvent the burglars. Perchance your wife needs a place to pack her bonnet in, and behold! there is the vase. . . . There is nothing like a vase, and this vase is the chief among ten thousand, and the one altogether costly. How Mr. Bryant managed to accept this elegant present without incidentally filling it with tears will forever be a mystery." (*The Rochester Democrat*, July 1876) In 1877 Bryant gave the vase to the Metropolitan Museum of Art.

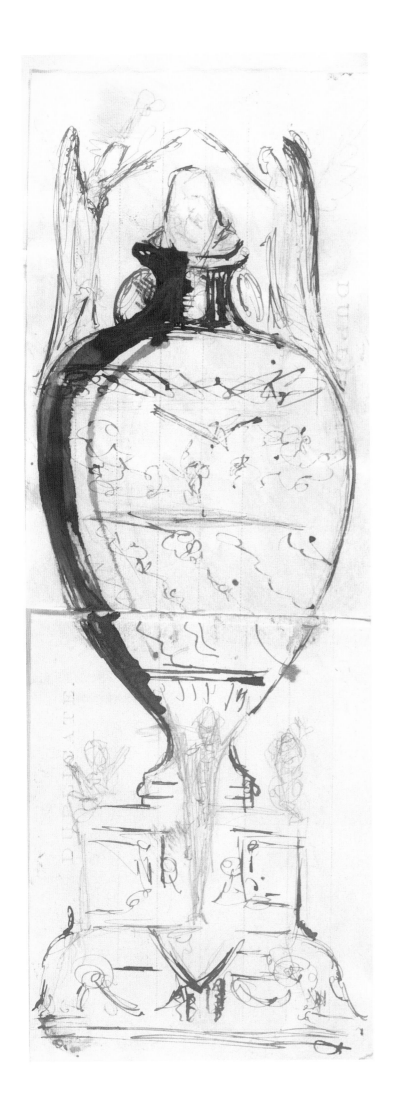

Eugene J. Soligny's preliminary suggestion for the Bryant Vase was surmounted by two angels holding laurels above a bust of William Cullen Bryant. The final version of the vase designed by Whitehouse retained the shape of the angels' wings as handles.

This massive 41½-inch-tall centerpiece, designed by James H. Whitehouse, was presented to construction manager Henry Meiggs (1811–1877) in commemoration of the completion of Peru's Mollendo-Arequipa railroad line in January 1871. When it was completed in June 1871, Tiffany's displayed it at its Union Square store. Under the headline "A Thing of Beauty," *The Evening Post* reported, "At the four angles of the base are the figures of Peruvian laborers, 'peons' of the country, in their native costume, with picks and spades at hand. . . . the whole is surmounted by the genius of Peru, a noble figure, bearing in one hand a rudder as the symbol of guidance, and in another a winged wheel typical of progress, with the rising sun at her feet." (June 9, 1871) Henry Meiggs made his first fortune in the lumber business during the California Gold Rush, and won election as an alderman of San Francisco, where he built California's first opera house and what is now Fishermen's Wharf. But he suffered drastic reverses due to a collapse in the real estate market in 1854, staving off his creditors with forged promissory notes that he stole from the city treasurer's office. Just as he was about to be exposed, Meiggs chartered a ship and sailed off with his family and $10,000 in gold. Landing in Chile, he found work as a railroad construction superintendent. The Chilean government gave him a contract to complete the Santiago-Valparaíso line over mountainous terrain; he completed the job in two years and made a million dollars. Peru was eager to build railroads rivaling Chile's, and Meiggs laid 1,042 miles of railroad in Peru in 1868–75: one of his high-altitude tunnels was said to "break the backbone of the Andes" and one of his trestles was called an "engineering wonder of the world." Meiggs satisfied most of his San Francisco debts, and the California legislature passed a law prohibiting grand juries from indicting him for offenses committed before 1855. When Peru collapsed into de facto bankruptcy in 1876, Meiggs devised a plan to rescue Peru's (and his own) fortunes by developing copper mines at Cerro de Pasco, but he died before the scheme could be implemented. Several years later, a syndicate of wealthy New Yorkers took over most of the Cerro de Pasco mines, whose revenues grew to over $100 million annually.

An 1871 photograph of the Meiggs Testimonial in its original state, before two of the arms had been removed.

The 15-inch-tall cup given to Queen Wilhelmina of the Netherlands on her marriage to Duke Henry of Mecklenburg-Schwerin by the Saint Nicholas Society, whose members are descended from immigrants to New Netherland (later New York). The royal couple's wedding took place on February 7, 1901, but the Saint Nicholas Society did not receive the queen's permission to present the cup until late January. Tiffany's completed the cup in March, and the Saint Nicholas Society presented it to Baron W. A. F. Gevers, minister of the Netherlands to the United States, at a banquet at Delmonico's Restaurant on April 8; among the more than 150 attendees was Professor Woodrow Wilson of Princeton, who was elected President of the United States eleven years later. The decoration of the cup commemorates the Dutch role in the history of New York: the most prominent figure is Saint Nicholas, the sixth-century bishop associated with Christmas gift-giving who became the city's patron saint. The man with the globe is Henry Hudson, the Englishman in Dutch employ who discovered New York for Europeans in September 1609. The peg-legged man is Peter Stuyvesant, director-general of New Netherland from 1647 until the British took over the colony in 1664, and the fourth figure (on the reverse side) is Admiral Cornelis Evertsen, commander of the Dutch squadron that recaptured New York in the summer of 1673. (This restoration was short-lived: as part of the settlement of the long war, the Dutch ceded the colony back to the British in 1674.)

In 1879 several Episcopalian bishops and the clergy of the Diocese of New York commissioned Tiffany's to make a 15-by-11-inch steel "casket" (box) to honor Right Reverend Horatio Potter on his twenty-fifth anniversary as Bishop of New York. Designed by James H. Whitehouse, it is decorated with silver symbols of the four Evangelists, Potter's gold portrait medallion on the front (probably by Eugene J. Soligny), and a gold finial representing the Bible, the cross, and the dove. Although the casket had not yet been completed, on November 25, 1879, it was presented to Potter in an elaborate choral ceremony at the Academy of Music (a predecessor of the Metropolitan Opera). This ceremony was a undoubtedly a competitive response to the dedication of the Roman Catholic St. Patrick's Cathedral on May 25, 1879. There was no Episcopalian cathedral in New York, and it was Potter who initiated the movement to build the Cathedral of St. John the Divine. This cathedral, designed to be the largest in the world apart from St. Peter's in Rome, remains uncompleted to this day. The casket was completed in April 1880, when Tiffany's exhibited it at its Union Square store. *The Evening Post* commented, "It is a most original and elaborate specimen of the goldsmith's art, and it is believed that no better workmanship can be produced anywhere abroad. . . . It is an interesting and agreeable fact that all the money paid for this gift and much more went directly to the workmen, and that not one dollar of profit remains to Tiffany & Co., who are content with the honor of the enterprise." (April 6, 1880) Potter's daughter, Mrs. Eli Chauncey, inherited the casket and donated it to the Cathedral of St. John the Divine in 1931.

In 1875 Reuben R. Springer, a retired Cincinnati merchant, proposed the construction of a music hall in Cincinnati to house the city's annual music festivals and industrial exhibitions. The magnificent Ruskinian Gothic structure eventually cost $300,000, of which Springer contributed $185,000 and Cincinnati citizens the remainder. In an intermission during the opening ceremonies on May 14, 1878, the hall's trustees presented Springer with this 17-inch-tall vase and accompanying dedicatory medal. Designed by James Whitehouse in the form of an ancient Greek amphora, closely echoing Whitehouse's Bryant Vase of 1876, the vase is decorated with lyres and olive branches, and has anthemion borders on the lip and foot. The surface, however, is hand hammered, a characteristic of Tiffany's Japanesque silver after 1876, and the horizontal band above the foot includes stylized chrysanthemums, symbols of the Emperor of Japan.

Yorktown Centennial Cup, 1881. Designed by James H. Whitehouse, its bas-reliefs and standing figure at the top were probably modeled and chased by Eugene J. Soligny. It commemorates the surrender of British troops to George Washington at Yorktown, Virginia, on October 19, 1781. The surrender brought down Lord North's intransigently anti-rebel British government and led to the Treaty of Paris, by which the British ceded the thirteen American colonies in 1783.

Frédéric-Auguste Bartholdi's Statue of Liberty was financed by a French public subscription as a centennial gift to the United States. The statue's arm and torch were displayed at the 1876 Centennial Exposition in Philadelphia in an effort to persuade the American public to subscribe to the construction of its pedestal in New York Harbor, but funds trickled in very slowly. In 1883 the Hungarian-born Joseph Pulitzer (1847–1911) took over *The World* and soon made it New York's most successful newspaper by appealing to the city's growing immigrant population. One of its circulation-building tactics was the Pedestal Fund for the Statue of Liberty, which was so successful that in 1886 *The World* boasted that contributions to the fund "exceeded by a handsome amount the sum of $100,000 necessary for the completion of the work." The pedestal and the installation of the statue were completed in the fall of 1886, when Bartholdi came to New York for the festivities surrounding President Grover Cleveland's dedication on October 27. *The World* commissioned Tiffany's to make a testimonial in Bartholdi's honor; designed by James H. White-house, the huge (38-inch-tall) testimonial has a petrified-wood base supporting a revolving globe with the map of France in silver gilt; it is topped with a replica of the statue's hand and torch. The globe is inscribed on one side, "All Homage and Thanks to the GREAT SCULPTOR, BARTHOLDI," and on the other, "A Tribute from the New York WORLD and Over 121,000 Americans to AUGUSTE BARTHOLDI and the Great Liberty-Loving People of France, 1886." *The World* reported, "The design of the testimonial is conceived in a spirit of mingled boldness and delicacy, its various details blending in a most harmonious whole. The execution is artistic in the extreme, a fitting evidence of the taste and sentiment of the American people. . . . The design, according to Mr. Whitehouse, has a twofold object—first, as typifying the idea embodied in the statue "Liberty Enlightening the World," and second, as a lasting allegorical record of the service done by THE WORLD newspaper and the contributors to its fund." (*The World*, November 13, 1886)

MARCH 7th 1886

➥ Three-foot-tall punch bowl inscribed "March 7th 1861" and "March 7th 1886," commissioned by the employees of the Anheuser-Busch Brewery—best known for Budweiser beer—for the twenty-fifth (silver) wedding anniversary of Adolphus and Lilly Anheuser Busch, whose marriage had united their families' breweries to form Anheuser-Busch. At the rim, four young satyrs holding garlands of hops vines straddle beer kegs with the Anheuser-Busch trademark. The body has repoussé-chased clusters of hops vines and barley, and the foot has repoussé-chased hops sprays, trophies, and torches. It was most probably designed by James H. Whitehouse, with the satyrs modeled by Eugene J. Soligny. ➥

➥ Archival photograph of the loving cup made for the Prince of Wales in 1883. The body's repoussé decoration includes thistles for Scotland, shamrocks for Ireland, Tudor roses for England, and three ostrich plumes, the ancient device of the Prince of Wales. The three horn-shaped handles are a literal representation of the "eldest-son labels"—bands of three inverted "horns"—in the Prince of Wales's coat of arms, an arcane reference indicating that the cup was designed by Tiffany's heraldry expert, James H. Whitehouse. The bottom of the cup is inscribed, "To the Prince of Wales / Tiffany & Company Gold and Silversmiths / in grateful remembrance of his interest in their craft, 1883." Tiffany's had good reason to be grateful to the Prince for his widely publicized patronage at the 1878 Paris Exposition, where he purchased a gourd-shaped Japanesque piece, Edward C. Moore's "Olympian" flatware, and a Japanesque gold brooch for his wife, Princess Alexandra. The United States Commissioner-General escorted the Prince through the Exposition's American section and reported, "The Tiffany pavilion was the favorite resort of the royal President of the British Commission, the Prince of Wales, and his lovely Princess, who were enthusiastic in their admiration of what they called 'the American novelties.'" The present whereabouts of the cup is unknown. ➥

➥ This stupefying 45-inch-tall trophy was anonymously commissioned by "robber baron" Jay Gould (owner of the steam yacht *Atalanta*) as a challenge cup for steam yacht races sponsored by the American Yacht Club. Probably designed by Charles Osborne and James H. Whitehouse (who apparently did not collaborate on any other well-known trophy), it was completed in 1887 and received wide attention in the press. The above illustration appeared in *The Jewelers' Circular* and *Harper's Weekly,* which commented, "Its design is altogether original, and in a broad sense suggests steam, speed, and victory upon the sea. At the base are represented fire and water, typified by figures representing Pluto and Neptune, who, with hands clasped, unite in producing steam, which is seen rising from the lower part of the body of the piece. . . . The handles, decorated with sea-weed and other plants of the water, appear to be growing up the sides of the vase, and, turning gracefully toward the neck, they terminate with the young and pleasing heads which represent the children of Aeolus. The vase springs from a bold shell-like base, upon which is represented the ocean, among whose waves are seen in idealized form a propeller and other devices especially appropriate to steam yachts. It is surmounted by a beautiful female figure, which holds in one hand a shield bearing the wheel and flag which form a distinguishing device of the American Yacht Club, and in the other the laurel wreath of victory." Jay Gould's business practices made him very unpopular with his fellow millionaires, which may explain why the American Yacht Club never received a challenge for this cup. Tiffany's displayed it at the 1893 Chicago Exposition and the 1901 Buffalo Exposition; its whereabouts

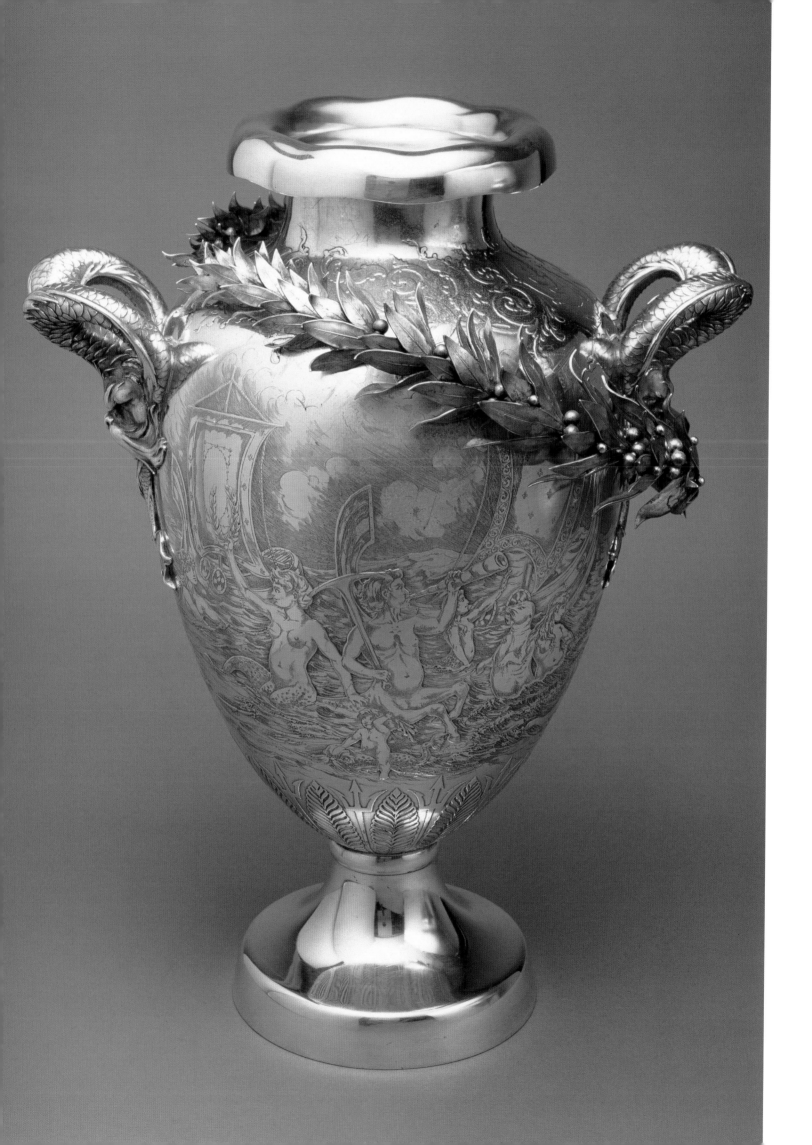

OPPOSITE:

⤜ James H. Whitehouse designed the 1892 Goelet Cup for Sloops. The 16½-inch-tall urn is engraved with scenes of satyrs and maidens at sea; the handles are supported by grotesque masks, and the shoulder has a removable laurel wreath. It was won by George C. Adams's *Harpoon*, skippered by his brother Charles Francis Adams, direct descendants of Presidents John and John Quincy Adams. Charles Francis Adams became one of America's leading yachtsmen. This trophy was exhibited at the 1893 Chicago Exposition, and it sold for $17,250 at Christie's on January 26, 1995. ⤛

⤜ This 18½-inch-long yachting trophy in the form of an oval punch bowl was made in 1896, and has bronze Native American warrior heads on each side. These heads were also used in 1896 for the handles of the Richard Croker cup (see page 109) and both pieces are attributable to James H. Whitehouse and Eugene J. Soligny. This was an international challenge trophy for a series of small yacht races sponsored by the Seawanhaka-Corinthian Yacht Club of Oyster Bay, New York. When *Munsey's Magazine* illustrated the trophy in its January 1901 issue, it was held by the Royal St. Lawrence Yacht Club of Canada. It sold at Sotheby's on January 21, 2000, for $85,000 and is now at the (Gene) Autry Museum of Western Heritage in Los Angeles. ⤛

James Gordon Bennett, publisher of the *Herald* in New York and Paris, continued to encourage yacht racing by commissioning this huge (19-inch-tall) $2,500 punch bowl as the prize for a thirty-mile race sailed in the Mediterranean off Nice on March 29, 1895. The competing yachts were the Prince of Wales's *Britannia* and the Scotch-brewing heir Andrew Barclay Walker's *Ailsa*, which won by two minutes and one second. Native American maidens decorate the base and form the handles, and each side of the bowl has "trophies" of Native American war regalia identical to those on the candelabra Bennett had commissioned to commemorate the *Dauntless*'s victory over the *Mohawk* in 1875 (see page 113) and the 1896 Croker cup (see page 109). James Gordon Bennett is best known for sending Henry Morton Stanley to find Dr. David Livingstone in Africa, but his career had many other facets. In 1876 he introduced polo to America at the Philadelphia Centennial Exhibition, and in 1880 he built the Newport Casino, home of American championship tennis from 1881 until 1915 and now the Tennis Hall of Fame. To break the transatlantic cable monopoly, in 1883 he and John W. Mackay (see page 148) founded the Commercial Cable Company, the predecessor of International Telephone and Telegraph. Bennett's personal behavior was sometimes outrageous: after one occasion—his fiancee's New Year's Day reception on January 1, 1877—she broke off their engagement, her brother horsewhipped him on the steps of the Union Club, and Bennett fought him in a duel to defend his honor (neither man was shot). Nevertheless, Bennett was reelected commodore of the New York Yacht Club in 1884. This trophy sold at Sotheby's for $167,500 on June 23, 1993.

Ogden Goelet was heir to an immense Manhattan real estate fortune that enabled his sister to marry the Duke of Roxburghe. In 1882 he established the Goelet Cups for schooner and sloop races held off Newport during the New York Yacht Club's annual cruises; the schooner trophies were valued at $1,000 each and the sloop trophies at $500 each. The thirty-two Goelet Cups awarded from 1882 until 1897 include many masterpieces of late-nineteenth-century design, many made by Tiffany's and some by the Whiting Manufacturing Co. This trophy, probably designed by James H. Whitehouse with Charles Osborne and Eugene J. Soligny, was won by Latham A. Fish's *Grayling* in the Goelet Cup schooner race sailed on August 8, 1884; the *Grayling* had capsized and sunk on her trial trip in 1883, and her victory was unexpected. Known as the Triton Cup, it is the most flamboyant trophy Tiffany's ever produced. Tiffany's displayed it at the 1893 Chicago Exposition.

This large (2-foot-tall) vase was presented to Willard A. Smith in commemoration of his organizing and supervising the construction of the Transportation Building at the 1893 World's Columbian Exposition in Chicago; the building's facade is represented on the front of the vase. Its overall composition and style suggest that it was designed by James H. Whitehouse. The Transportation Building, the only building at the Exposition that was not in the neoclassical style, was designed by the great architect Louis Sullivan (1856–1924). The monumental entrance of receding semicircular arches was Sullivan's homage to the semicircular arches characteristic of the work of architect H. H. Richardson (1838–1886). Louis Comfort Tiffany also used receding semicircular arches in the chapel he displayed at the Columbian Exposition. ABOVE: casting patterns for "Sea Transportation" and "Land Transportation," which appear on the opposite sides of the vase under the "wave" and "cloud" handles. RIGHT: allegorical representation of "Sea Transportation" on one side of the vase.

On July 1, 1899 President William McKinley presented this 13¾-inch-tall cup to French Ambassador Jules Cambon for his role in negotiating the truce that ended the Spanish–American War. By the terms of the peace treaty, signed in Paris on December 10, 1898, Spain ceded Cuba, Puerto Rico, Guam, and the Philippines to the United States. The scales on the body represent the breast armor of Minerva (goddess of wisdom and peace), the handles are decorated with olive leaves, and the beaks of the eagles on the base hold a laurel garland. The base is typical of the designs of James H. Whitehouse, who in 1884 designed the obverse of the Great Seal of the United States: the seal appears on this cup beneath the handle on the left; emblems of France and Spain are beneath the other two handles. The cup is now in the collection of the White House in Washington, D.C.

Archival photograph of the Croker Cup. In 1886 the Irish-born Richard Croker (1841–1922) became the leader of Tammany Hall, the chief bastion of Democratic Party strength in New York City. In contrast with his immediate predecessor, "Honest John" Kelly, Croker was openly corrupt: under his leadership Tammany's battle cry was "to Hell with the reformers." In 1894 Croker astounded New Yorkers by resigning from Tammany and moving to England, where he established himself as a race-horse breeder, but he nevertheless retained control of Tammany through his associates. When he visited New York in early 1896, Tammany demonstrated its fealty with a banquet and loving cup presentation at the Hotel Savoy on February 8. The rabidly anti-Tammany *New York Times* described the cup the next day, and its comments on the cup's beauty and artistry should not be taken at face value: "A beautiful silver loving cup presented to Mr. Croker will rank with many of the famous products shown at the World's Columbian Exposition. Studies of the native Indians were one of the features of their decorative silver at their Chicago exhibit, and as this subject was the keynote of the decoration in last night's testimonial, Tiffany & Co.'s artists were particularly well equipped for it. The cup weighs 210 ounces, stands 13½ inches high, and has a capacity of two gallons. It is a superb example of a massive piece of silverware, which, through the skillful treatment of the artists, chiefly suggests solidity combined with art, while its massiveness and weight is only revealed in its handling . . . in its entirety the cup is an example of the highest art work in silversmithing." (February 8) This cup's Native American imagery was particularly appropriate because Tammany was named for a supposed chief of the Delaware tribe. Tiffany's had used this cup's Native American trophies on the Bennett candelabra in 1875 (see page 113) and the Bennett punch bowl in 1894 (see page 104). Croker returned to New York in September 1897 and headed Tammany in person until he retired to Ireland five years later.

Inscribed "To Joseph E. Schwab from the Employees of the Duquesne Steel Works and Blast Furnaces June 1, 1901," the body of this three-handled, 15½-inch-tall cup is etched with steel-making scenes flanked by sculpted figures of a miner, a mill worker, and a draped female representing Earth. The body rests upon a globe, and three sculpted bald eagles rest upon the steel foot. Joseph Schwab (1864–1922) was a younger brother of Carnegie Steel president Charles Schwab (see caption at left), who in 1896 appointed him general supervisor of the Duquesne Works. Joe Schwab received $1 million for his Carnegie stock in the United States Steel buyout and used the money to establish himself as the leading options trader in New York. In 1907 he left his wife and children for a Broadway actress; after World War I he lost his fortune in an attempt to corner the wheat market; and in 1922 he died of drink. The cup sold at Sotheby's for $34,500 on January 20, 1998.

This loving cup was presented in 1901 to Charles M. Schwab (1862–1939), formerly president of Andrew Carnegie's steel company, in commemoration of his central role in consummating the $400 million sale of the company to the newly formed United States Steel Corporation, by far the largest merger of the time. The cup's three handles are winged dragons; the body has repoussé scenes of steel-making flanked by Vulcan and Mercury. Schwab was president of United States Steel from 1901 until 1904, when he resigned to take over the management of Bethlehem Steel, a company he had acquired as a personal investment in 1901. His reputation was tarnished by the bankruptcy of American Shipbuilding, a company formed to take over Bethlehem Steel, but he salvaged Bethlehem Steel from the American Shipbuilding wreckage and rehabilitated his reputation with the success of Bethlehem Steel's shipbuilding program for the United States Navy during World War I.

EUGENE JULIUS SOLIGNY

The most enigmatic of Tiffany's nineteenth-century silver designers, Eugene J. Soligny came to Tiffany & Co. shortly after James Whitehouse's arrival in 1858.

Soligny was born in Paris in May 1832 and evidently studied in Paris in the early- to mid-1850s with Léonard Morel-Ladeuil (1820–1888), the then much-admired metal sculptor and repoussé-work chaser who had previously studied and later collaborated with another prominent metal sculptor, Antoine Vechte (1799–1868).

Both Vechte and Ladeuil were to make significant contributions to the English neoclassic and neo-Renaissance styles; Vechte leaving France to work at Hunt & Roskell in London after the Paris Revolution of 1848, the same year he had received the Legion of Honor, and Ladeuil following him to England in 1859 to work at Elkington's. Vechte returned to France in 1861; Ladeuil, although he returned to France in 1885, would design for Elkington's until his death on March 15, 1888, at Boulogne-sur-Mer.

Soligny knew Ladeuil well, and his style, which remained obdurately revivalist and academic even if marvelously well-crafted, reflects Ladeuil's dedication to the neo-Renaissance Beaux-Arts style of the era of Napoleon III.

Soligny immigrated to the United States in 1856, when he was twenty-four, and was naturalized fifteen years later on April 26, 1871. Had he already in 1856 an offer of employment from Tiffany's? A highly talented young designer, sculptor, and silver chaser with excellent connections would have needed a major incentive to leave the lavishness of Second Empire Paris in its heyday for the relative austerity of pre–Civil War New York.

It is highly probable that Edward C. Moore and Gideon Reed would have visited the celebrated Ladeuil on their scouting trip to Paris in 1855 and would have not only studied his teaching methods but met his pupil Soligny. Moore clearly scrutinized Elkington's progress, and Elkington's obviously followed Ladeuil's career and decided to hire him in 1859. Had Moore in 1855 discussed employment at Tiffany & Co. with both Ladeuil and Soligny? It would be surprising if he had not. Ladeuil was one of Paris's leading metalsmiths and academic sculptors of that time, known since the Paris Salon

A pair of six-light candelabra commissioned by *New York Herald* publisher James Gordon Bennett to commemorate the race between his 121-foot *Dauntless* and William T. Garner's 141-foot *Mohawk* outside New York Harbor on October 26, 1875; the *Dauntless* won and Bennett used the $2,000 prize (to which both men had contributed $1,000) to commission these candelabra from Tiffany's. They symbolized Bennett's victory: the exultant Native American warriors at the tops brandishing knives and scalps represent the *Dauntless*, and the glum warriors paddling the birchbark canoes represent the *Mohawk*. Native American "trophies"—bison heads and bison hooves supporting the base—carry out the theme. Eight months after the race, Americans were horrified by the news that Garner, his wife, and four guests were drowned when the *Mohawk* capsized and sank at its mooring in a freak accident at Stapleton, Staten Island, on July 20, 1876. The candelabra were shown by Tiffany's at the Philadelphia Centennial Exhibition of 1876 and the Paris Exposition Universelle of 1878, when the London *Spectator* noted their "strictly American character and design." (September 21, 1878) However, the French critic Emile Bergerat commented snidely, "The arms of the Savages of the North, their hairstyles, their insignia of war or peace, furnish the decorative designs of this candelabrum. It is moreover of a purely American character, and it indicates their origin and their destination." (*Les chefs-d'oeuvre d'art à l'Exposition Universelle;* 1878) In 1880 Tiffany's made a second pair of these candelabra for Mary Jane Morgan (see page 150); this pair was purchased for $3,500 at the March 10, 1886, auction of Mrs. Morgan's silver by Mrs. G. W. Quintard, Mrs. Morgan's stepdaughter. The auction catalogue attributed them to the celebrated American sculptor Augustus Saint-Gaudens, but these warriors bear no resemblance to the nobility and quiet dignity of Saint-Gaudens's other sculpture, and were most likely the work of Eugene J. Soligny.

⤳ A sketch of a Native American paddling a canoe from Eugene J. Soligny's sketchbook for the Bennett Candelabra on page 113. ⤳

of 1853 where he exhibited a richly damascened iron and silver allegorical shield commissioned by no less a celebrity than the Emperor Napoleon III himself.

There are no records of the date of Soligny's first employment at Tiffany's, however, somewhere in late 1858 would be sufficiently accurate. A drawing in Soligny's portfolio in the Tiffany Archives is dated "Richmond 1859," indicating that he was then living in New York's Richmond County (Staten Island). Richmond had a considerable French Huguenot population at the time, and it was not inconvenient to Tiffany's Prince Street silver manufactory, the Staten Island & New York Ferry Co. having been providing hourly service between Whitehall Street and Port Richmond since 1853.

The drawings in the Tiffany Archives are dated from 1859 to 1866 and most are in the elaborate Napoleon III neo-Renaissance revivalist mode popularized in America by imports from Elkington's, as well as by both Gorham's designs by George Wilkinson and Tiffany's designs by James H. Whitehouse and, it seems safe to add, by Eugene J. Soligny.

Surviving photographs of Tiffany's wares for the Paris Exposition of 1867 include, along with Moore's Saracenic tea set, three elaborate pieces in a mixed neoclassic/neo-Renaissance style: a water pitcher, a decorative urn with mask handles, and a footed compote with an elaborately chased frieze and angular neoclassic handles. All three combine the severity of form and exquisite detailing of Whitehouse design, but the masks of the urn's handles and the elaborately chased friezes of the pitcher and compote have a neo-Renaissance flamboyance foreign to Whitehouse (and certainly to Moore) that would suggest the hand of Soligny in their creation.

In 1867 Soligny's initials appear for the first time on a piece of Tiffany silver, the Westchester Cup. Soligny notes that James Whitehouse was the designer of the cup but that he did the chasing. Did he also sculpt the final figures: the horses and jockeys, the midnight Halloween chase, and the Indian? Whitehouse was an engraver, silver designer, and intaglio gem cutter, but nothing indicates that he was a sculptor. There is also a preliminary sketch for the Indian atop the Jerome Park Cup amongst Soligny's drawings, so it is almost certain that he sculpted as well as chased all the figures on all three levels of the Jerome Park Cup.

The next signed work by Soligny is the repoussé panel of the racehorse on the front of the Comanche Trophy commissioned by August Belmont in 1873. Again, is Soligny's signature for the horse panel alone or did he sculpt the running horse and its Comanche warrior rider atop the trophy as well? His sketchbook in the Tiffany Archives includes preliminary studies for both.

Soligny would, of course, never have seen a Comanche warrior, but he may well have seen explorer-painter Alfred Jacob Miller's paintings of Western Indians of the late 1860s, including one titled *Dodging an Arrow (Crows)* now in the Walters Art Gallery. Miller wrote in reference to this painting that shows an Indian warrior in the same daredevil battle position as the "Comanche" Indian of the Tiffany trophy: "In skirmishing on horseback, [the Indian] makes a target of his horse, watching the deadly arrow of his adversary;—he quick as lightning clings to his horse's neck;—dropping his body to the opposite side, exposing but a part of his arm and leg to his enemy—sometimes he holds on simply by the heel while, the horse is in full motion. In such an attitude he will discharge his arrows under the horse's neck, recovering his seat in a moment;—this is only attained by long practice,—a broken neck certainly awaits any one who tries to accomplish the feat for the first time."

Soligny very probably also had as a reference the 1837 *Catalogue of Catlin's Indian Gallery of Portraits, Landscapes, Manners and Customs, etc.* whose 494 pictures included another

⤜ Pencil self-portrait of Eugene J. Soligny at about age twenty-four. This drawing is in a Soligny sketchbook in the Tiffany Archives dating from circa 1876, but it appears to be his image of himself more than twenty years earlier, when he was still living in Paris. ⤛

Commodore's Challenge Cup for Schooners, commissioned by New York Yacht Club Commodore James Gordon Bennett in 1871. It was probably designed by James H. Whitehouse and modeled and chased by Eugene J. Soligny. Eighteen schooners competed in the first race, sailed in New York harbor on June 22, 1871; it was won by William Voorhis's *Tidal Wave*. The second race, sailed off Newport two months later, was won by R. F. Loper's *Madgie*. The last race for this cup was sailed in 1901.

Soligny's sketch for a preliminary version of the National Cup for Stallions.

The National Cup for Stallions, designed by James H. Whitehouse and Eugene Soligny, was commissioned in 1876 for the inaugural Breeder's Trotting Meeting held in Philadelphia. When Tiffany's exhibited the 21½-inch-long trophy at its store in August, *The Spirit of the Times* reported: "Its design is both elegant and appropriate, and is manufactured and finished in the high style for which the skilled art of that great house has become world-famous. . . . The upper part of the bowl is encircled by a border of horse-shoes, entwined with laurel. The two heavy handles are of chased castings, as are likewise the horses' heads, which spring from the sides of the bowl, decorated at the joining with laurel. The richly cast and chased base is supported by four massive feet, upon which is laid a large horse-shoe of oxydized silver, and a sprig of laurel, emblems of the flying hoof, and the victory won." This was the first important trotting trophy. *The Spirit of the Times* commented: "On the trotting turf we have not known this form of awarding prizes, because this great sport is still in its infancy. The trotting horse is yet in a crude state so far as his breeding is concerned, but out of the conglomerate mass that training and the turf has thrown to the surface, we begin to see well-defined lines of blood that are rising into superior place. . . . The Breeders' Meeting of our Centennial year is the first united action of the American breeders of trotting horses. . . . The event will be remembered for all time as the inauguration of a new system of racing upon the trotting turf, and will be associated with the Centennial year as marking a new era in trotting history." (August 19, 1876) It was won by A. J. McKimmin's Blackwood, Jr., at Philadelphia's Suffolk Park on October 2, 1876.

The first Westminster Kennel Club dog show (seen in the illustration at left) was held in May 1877 at Gilmore's Garden, which in 1883 was renamed Madison Square Garden, the first of four facilities of that name where the Westminster Kennel Club has continued to hold its annual shows. Tiffany & Co. made all the trophies awarded at the first 1877 show. This trophy, valued at $150 and donated by the New York City Association for the Protection of Game, was offered at the 1877 show for the best brace of setters. Several drawings of setters in Eugene J. Soligny's sketchbooks at Tiffany's Archives—particularly the one at the upper right closely resembling the setter depicted at the top of this trophy—suggest that Soligny designed this trophy and based the setter on his own dog. The trophy, which originally had a large marble base with an applied silver "trophy" of hunting gear, was won by the red-and-white English setters Nip and Tuck, owned by Mrs. R. A. McCurdy of New York City. Mrs. McCurdy was a forebear of the George Robert Leslie family, in whose hands the trophy remained until 1999, when Mrs. George Robert Leslie returned it to the Westminster Kennel Club.

version of this unusual battle position in an illustration titled *Comanche Feats of Horsemanship* (1834–35). (The painting is now in the Smithsonian Institution.) In his *Letters and Notes* George Catlin wrote:

> Amongst their feats of riding, there is one that has astonished me more than anything of the kind I have ever seen, or expect to see, in my life:—a strategem of war, learned and practiced by every young man in the tribe; by which he is able to drop his body upon the side of his horse at the instant he is passing, effectually screened from his enemies' weapons as he lays in a horizontal position behind the body of his horse, with his heel hanging over the horses' back; by which he has the power of throwing himself up again, and changing to the other side of the horse if necessary. In this wonderful condition, he will hang whilst his horse is at fullest speed, carrying with him his bow and his shield, and also his long lance of fourteen feet in length, all or either of which he will wield upon his enemy as he passes; rising and throwing his arrows over the horse's back, or with equal ease and equal success under the horse's neck.

Miller was decidedly better at rendering horses in motion than Catlin. Neither, however, was at the level of the rendering of the galloping horse of the Tiffany trophy, which has astonishing vigor in its movement.

There have been suggestions that the great Irish-French-American sculptor Augustus Saint-Gaudens (1848–1907) had a hand in the Comanche warrior; however, the young Saint-Gaudens, although he did sculpt the legendary Indian Chief Hiawatha in Rome between 1872 and 1874, depicted him in a pondering, meditative, seated pose with no hint of the agitated, dramatic action of the Comanche warrior figure in question. During Saint-Gaudens's stay in Rome, his work—strongly neoclassic and serene—was under the influence of the greats of neoclassicism Antonio Canova (1757–1822) and Bertel Thorwaldsen (1770–1844), rather than under that of the American West's lesser- to little-known explorer-painters. The Comanche Trophy's horse and warrior, totally out of keeping with Saint-Gaudens's style of 1873, appear to be Eugene J. Soligny's work. Unless other contenders are discovered, it is his masterpiece.

Two years later, Soligny and Saint-Gaudens would apparently collaborate with James H. Whitehouse on a piece of

Designed by Eugene J. Soligny in 1873, this table centerpiece was prominently displayed at the 1876 Centennial Exhibition in Philadelphia. A critic for *The Art Journal* sternly disapproved of its design, writing that it "is so elaborated as to sacrifice much of grace—it is indeed, an effort at peculiarity. It is said to have been 'studied from the Syrian style,' but it is a style to be avoided rather than imitated." (*The Art Journal*, 1876)

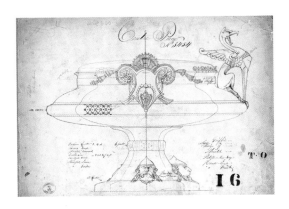

A working drawing of the centerpiece shown in the illustration on the opposite page.

presentation silver, the Bryant Vase. Soligny's signature appears on the superbly chased profile portrait of the poet in the principal medallion on the front of the vase; Saint-Gaudens's records indicate he provided the models for the remaining five bas-relief medallions on the vase. Soligny, it appears, chased all the medallions as well as the rest of the vase after James Whitehouse's designs; and to Soligny's great credit, the Bryant Vase remains the greatest work of repoussé chasing made in America.

Soligny very possibly also had a hand in sculpting the extravagant American Indian Candelabra made for James Gordon Bennett, owner of the *New York Herald* in 1875. Saint-Gaudens (although it is as atypical of his work as the Comanche warrior) is credited with sculpting the ferocious scalps- and knife-brandishing warrior in the full heat of his war dance that crowns these daunting, aggressively Americanized Elkingtonesque silver constructions of spears, shields, bison heads, canoes, bison hooves, feathers, scalps, and Indians. (Note that Edward C. Moore has been credited with the overall design even though it bears no resemblance to his style and fits perfectly with the compositional style of James Whitehouse.)

In her 1969 biography of Saint-Gaudens—much of which she bases on *The Reminiscences of Augustus Saint-Gaudens,* edited and liberally amplified by his son Homer in 1913, six years after the sculptor's death—Louise Tharp notes: "For Tiffany, Gus modeled a candelabra, the figure of an Indian dancing with knife and scalp. It was to be rendered in silver for Gordon Bennett, who planned to award it as a prize in a race sponsored by the New York Yacht Club. This order, too, was finished and paid for in New York. Now and for many years to come, Saint-Gaudens found Tiffany a good firm to deal with." No mention is made of the more peaceable Indian paddling his canoe between the cloven-hooved bison feet of the yachting trophy candelabrum. This rather static Indian is more likely by Soligny than Saint-Gaudens, an attribution encouraged by numerous studies of Indians paddling canoes in Soligny's sketchbooks.

The sculpting of the bison head, the war trophy, and the hooves is also most probably by Soligny. In any case, the Bennett candelabra, although admired in their time, are so aesthetically corrupt and conceptually preposterous that they are a credit to no one despite their intriguing Victorian eccentricity and eclecticism—a case of "too many cooks"; and, in any case, they are currently lost, nothing remaining save poor contemporary illustrations and photographs to judge whatever redeeming qualities they may have had.

They, along with the more successful Comanche Trophy and the extraordinary Bryant Vase, were displayed by Tiffany's at the Philadelphia Centennial Exposition of 1876 and again at the Paris Exposition of 1878.

The surviving photograph of Tiffany's silver display at the 1876 Philadelphia Exposition features a large silver-and-niello salver picturing a young woman of the French Renaissance (termed "in the style of Henri II") listening to the whispers of a pair of cupids that hover one by each ear. The salver bears the old French legend *"Lequel des deux éscouteray-je?"* ("Which of the two shall I listen to?")

This mysterious salver is explained by the fact that Soligny's mentor, Léonard Morel-Ladeuil, showed a twenty-inch diameter silver, gold, and steel repoussé plaque of a "Pompeian Lady at her Toilet" in the Elkington display at the Philadelphia Centennial, along with his Helicon Vase and a facsimile of his Milton Shield shown in Paris in 1867. It is more than likely that Soligny would have had word of Ladeuil's lengthy preparations for the exhibit and prepared his answer to Ladeuil's "Pompeian Lady" with his own Renaissance lady with its legend. Again Soligny's sketchbooks provide a key in a satirical cartoon of two dandies examining a large salver hanging in a gallery. The image on the salver is a giant fish, and the legend does not read "Which one shall I listen to?" but "Which one shall I swallow?" (*"Lequel des deux avalarai-je?"*)

Also shown in Philadelphia, but not particularly to Soligny's credit, was the 1873 design of a "Syrian Urn Centerpiece. Its dubious effect was compounded by six additional pieces of a dessert service. All inexplicably combined snarling female griffins with ancient Assyrian masks. Tiffany's catalogue described this unfortunate effort of Soligny's as an "Assyrian Dessert Service of seven pieces, embracing the repoussé and appliqué processes, tinted by treatment with oxide of gold." *The Art Journal* of 1876 dismissed it as "an effort at peculiarity. It is said to have been 'studied from the Syrian style,' but it is a style to be avoided rather than imitated."

The quality of hand-drawn illustrations of objects at the 1876 Exposition being poor at best, it is impossible to positively identify Soligny's hand in other trophies exhibited by

☙ Eugene J. Soligny's circa 1865 design
for a compote decorated with fruits and
birds. ☙

Tiffany's that might well have been further collaborations of Whitehouse and Soligny. Prominent candidates would include the highly praised Centennial Cup with a repoussé panel of George Washington on horseback leading his troops into battle and, by report, a remarkably beautifully crafted figural group of Washington standing beside a mare and her foal; repoussé picture on the front of the Ocean Challenge Cup's depicting a scene from Longfellow's "Wreck of the *Hesperus*"; and finally the vigorous horse heads on the National Cup for Stallions. It is abundantly clear from stylistic evidence, however, that Whitehouse and Soligny were lifelong collaborators on Tiffany trophies, almost all of which they designed from the 1860s to the 1890s.

If Soligny made important contributions to the Paris Exposition of 1878, beyond a small series of intricately chased allegorical salvers, they are unrecorded, though in 1878 he was recognized and greatly praised as the chaser of the Bryant Vase electroformed replica shown at the fair. Tiffany's, of course, won the grand prize for silver, and several of its craftsmen were recognized with medals as well. However, the *New York Sun* of September 8, 1878, recorded: "A curious fact in connection with these awards is that Mr. Soligny, the best and highest paid chaser whom Messrs. Tiffany employ, has not received any reward at all. The reason of it is that, being a Frenchman, he works in the classical old style. His works are excellent, but there is nothing new in his process, and the jury did not think him more deserving of a reward than any of the distinguished chasers Paris can boast of." This must have come as a severe disappointment to Soligny, especially in view of the fact that his old teacher Léonard Morel-Ladeuil, who also worked "in the classical old style," was given the Legion of Honor in 1878 for his own work for Elkington's.

That same year Soligny worked with Whitehouse on another important commemorative work, the Nast Testimonial Vase, for which he again provided and signed the central hand-chased figural medallion, as well as on a large bas-relief plaque completed in 1879 of Indians on horseback hunting bison. In November 1879, the *National Repository* termed this "Military and Naval Challenge Trophy" "a master work of repoussé chasing in black steel," and "the fairest metallic art work of [this] land and time." Related in overall style was his last signed work, the 1884 superbly chased portrait medallion of James J. Hill, the prominent Minneapolis businessman and railroad tycoon, on an elaborate presentation plaque. Again there is no record of his contributions to Tiffany's silver displayed in Paris in 1889, where Tiffany's again won the grand prize.

In 1890 Soligny became the foreman of Tiffany's chasing department and in 1893 was the foreman for the production of silver for the World's Columbian Exposition. His exact contributions to the creation of the silver pieces shown in Chicago in 1893 went unrecorded, although they were surely many. And of his work during the remainder of the 1890s, there is again no information; nor is there for his participation, if any, in Tiffany's grand prize–winning silver display at the Paris Exposition of 1900. In June of 1894 he apparently fell into disfavor at Tiffany's; the firm voided his bonus contract.

Eugene Soligny died in Brooklyn on January 10, 1901, at the age of sixty-eight. No other silversmith in Tiffany's history has had his work held in such high regard as to be allowed to place his signature on Tiffany silver. Even the great Augustus Saint-Gaudens, if he indeed produced sculpted silver figures for Tiffany's, did not sign them.

Soligny was paid, according to contemporary records, more than three times the salary of other Tiffany silver chasers. Whitehouse chose him to collaborate on his most important commemorative pieces. His chasing of the Bryant Vase remains to this day the most important example of repoussé work executed in America.

How peculiar that recent scholarship persists in trying to take credit from Soligny and offer it to Saint-Gardens, not based on any credible stylistic similarity between the two artists' work, but on long-after-the-fact and highly inaccurate reminiscences of Edward C. Moore's younger brother, Thomas, who was a classmate at Cooper Union and friend of Saint-Gaudens, and other distant reminiscences of Saint-Gaudens's son, Homer, neither an impartial observer.

That Augustus Saint-Gaudens was a better artist and sculptor, of that there is no doubt; but Soligny's work too deserves its own place of certain honor in the history of American design.

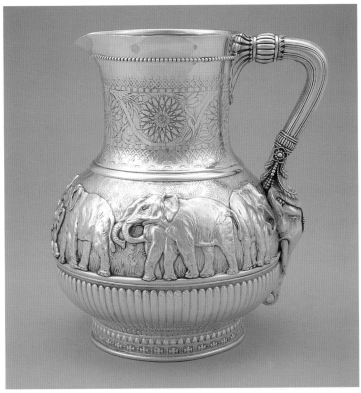

Footed bowl in the Indian style with cast handles representing caparisoned elephant heads. Tiffany's ledgers show that it was made on September 11, 1874, with a manufacturing cost of $128, and that other versions were made with additional chasing; their manufacturing costs ranged as high as $250. Stylistically it is close to the highly detailed and eclectic silverwares produced by Elkington's of Birmingham, England. This similarity suggests that it could well have been designed by James Whitehouse, although the elephant handles are typical of Eugene Soligny's work in the early 1870s.

Circa 1874 Indian-style pitcher with an elephant-head handle and a frieze of bas-relief elephants. It was probably designed by James H. Whitehouse and modeled and chased by Eugene J. Soligny.

THIS PAGE AND OPPOSITE:

In 1871 the United States government sued the British Crown under international law for breaching its neutrality during the Civil War by building five warships for the Confederacy. The governments agreed to have the case decided by a board of three arbitrators from neutral countries. The board met in Geneva in the winter of 1871–72, found that Britain had violated its neutrality, and ordered Britain to pay reparations of $15 million. The U.S. Department of State then commissioned Tiffany's to produce elaborate silver services for each of the arbitrators, Viscount d'Itajubá of Brazil, Count Sclopsis of Italy, and Jacques Staempfli of Switzerland. Each service comprised a punch bowl 26½ inches in diameter, a pair of 30½-inch-tall candelabra, and a pair of 13¼-inch-tall wine coolers. One of the services was exhibited at Tiffany's store after it was completed, and the *Brooklyn Daily Argus* described it as having "contrasts of effect [achieved] by opposing oxidized reliefs to satin-finished and burnished surfaces, with points brightened by gilding. On the wine-coolers two of the sides are decorated with figures in relief, emblematic of Commerce and Agriculture. . . . Yet the designer has appreciated the material in which he was working, and, instead of copying the flowing lines of marble drapery, has broken it here into unstudied horizontal lines. And the same criticism, with the same praise, may be justly given to the female figure that supports the candelabrum. . . . Putting on one side the designing, an artist will most conscientiously praise the exquisite workmanship. The terminal human heads, the beading, the scroll-work, the vine-leaves and grapes of the vase [punch bowl], and the figures and decorations of the candelabra and wine-coolers, are certainly perfectly wrought." (Tiffany Archives) The candelabra's figures of Ariadne (wife of Dionysus, whose head was used for the handles of the punch bowl) were signed by Eugene J. Soligny, who must have designed the entire service, which probably did not please his English-born collaborator James H. Whitehouse. One of the services was again exhibited at the Vienna Exposition of 1873. The service illustrated here was presented to Viscount d'Itajubá in Paris by State Department representative E. B. Washburne in March 1873 and is now at the Art Institute of Chicago. Jacques Staempfli's service is now at the Musée d'Art et d'Histoire in Geneva. A matching punch bowl was offered at Sotheby's on January 20, 1996 (with an estimate of $50,000–$70,000) but was not sold.

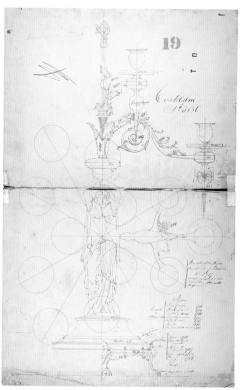

125

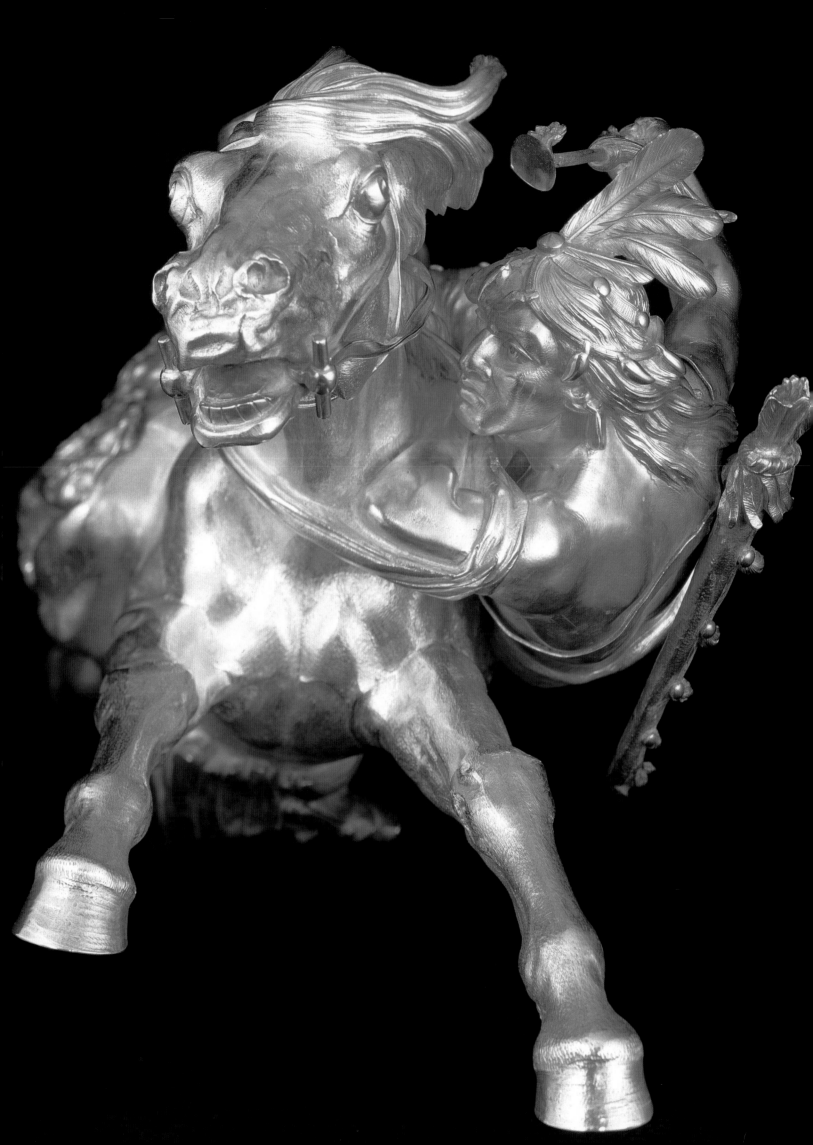

Tiffany's records show that the Comanche Trophy was commissioned in 1873 by August Belmont, who probably intended it for the 1873 running of the Belmont Stakes (which he had founded in 1867), but another trophy featuring Native American warriors was awarded instead. Eugene J. Soligny placed his initials on the bas-relief horse at the base of the Comanche Trophy, and it is believed that he also modeled the horse and rider, one of the most striking works of nineteenth-century American sculpture. Tiffany's showed it at the 1876 Centennial Exhibition in Philadelphia, and one critic deemed it the best piece in the exhibit (Phillip T. Sandhurst, *The Great Centennial Exhibition Critically Described and Illustrated,* 1876). It is inscribed "L.J.P. to R.B., January 1, 1874"; L. J. P. was probably Lewis J. Powell, a Springfield, Massachusetts, paper manufacturer who founded the Hampden Park trotting horse racetrack, and R. B. was Robert Bonner, a wealthy New York magazine publisher and trotting horse fancier. Bonner's religious scruples against betting prevented him from entering his horses in races, but at the Lexington, Kentucky, Fair Grounds on November 11, 1884, he ran his trotter, Maud S., in a one-horse exhibition over a mile-long course; several churchmen attended to make sure that no betting occurred. Maud S. beat her own record of 2:09:45 to finish in 2:09:15, and Bonner was presented with the Woodburn Farm Cup made by Tiffany's. LEFT: Soligny's sketches of Native American hunters on horseback.

In 1876 August Belmont, president of the American Jockey Club, commissioned the Centennial Cup for a commemorative race at Jerome Park. *The New York Herald*'s turf reporter described it as "a group of statuary in silver, with highly ornamental bas-reliefs upon the sides and ends of the dark marble base. . . . It was designed by Mr. J. H. Whitehouse and it represents a scene described by Washington Irving. The group represents [George] Washington making a call upon one of his thoroughbred brood mares and her colt foal. Washington stands with one hand resting on the back of his old friend, the mare, and the other extended toward his young friend, the colt foal. The colt appears to be a little stiff in posture but this is natural, perhaps, as he is dropping himself away from his owner's hand. The figure of Washington is chaste, faithful, lifelike, just what the people want to see. The ease, the dignity and the lofty character of the great man are beautifully blended with his well known love for horses. One of the bas-reliefs depicts Washington leading his infantry in a charge at the battle of Princeton. The other represents his reception at Trenton by girls and women." (October 13, 1876) The bas-reliefs and sculpted figures can be attributed to Eugene J. Soligny, although the overall design is characteristic of James H. Whitehouse. The four-mile race was run before ten thousand spectators on October 12: the *Tribune* reported, "Tom Ochiltree, who won the beautiful trophy for the well-known turfman, George L. Lorillard, never before looked more thoroughly like a great racer. Acrobat, although unable to compel Ochiltree to show the fullest extent of his powers, nevertheless made a proud record for himself, astonished everyone by an exhibition of pluck and endurance, while carrying six pounds more weight than Ochiltree, and clung tenaciously to the great racer's flank as the two crossed the score. The time, 7 minutes and 30 seconds, was very fast for the course." (October 13, 1876) George Lorillard and his better-known older brother Pierre (founder of Tuxedo Park) were heirs to a long-established tobacco fortune, and both were renowned turfmen, yachtsmen, carriage drivers, and trap shooters. George was thirty-three years old when Tom Ochiltree (one of his first horses) won the Centennial Cup. In subsequent years his horses won the Preakness Stakes five times in succession (starting in 1878), Monmouth Park's Hopeful States four times in succession, the Dixie Stakes three times, and the Vernal Stakes five times; they also had four victories each in the Juvenile Stakes and the Baltimore Cup. The whereabouts of this great work of Tiffany silversmithing is unknown, and there is no surviving photograph in the Tiffany Archives.

✍ Archival photograph of the Military and Naval Challenge Trophy commissioned by former judge Henry Hilton as the first prize for Army, Navy, National Guard, and foreign sharp-shooting teams in the National Rifle Association's annual match at Creedmore near Queens Village on Long Island. The first Challenge match took place on September 21, 1878, and was won by the New York State team: at the award ceremony the trophy was represented by a drawing because Tiffany's had not completed it. It was completed in May 1879, when it was illustrated and described in *The Spirit of the Times*: "The Trophy itself is a unique work, and possesses many attractive qualities to commend it to connoisseurs and art lovers, apart from its higher interest as an emblem of victory. The form is that of a shield, an irregular, oblong shape, drooping like a curtain. The centre presents a superb picture, in *repoussé* steel, of an Indian buffalo hunt. In the foreground are three Indian riders, mounted on their spirited ponies are pursuing with bow and lance the leaders of a herd of buffaloes, which extends in interminable numbers, far away in the distance. The action of horse and rider is admirably expressed, and the headlong fright and fury of the hunted brutes shown with striking reality. . . . The whole design is surmounted by a sculpted eagle, and in the detail of the ornament, silver, copper, gold, and the new Japanese metal [*mokume*], which has lately been developed, here are successfully employed." (May 17) The overall design is by James H. Whitehouse and the masterfully chased buffalo hunt is the work of Eugene J. Soligny, whose notebooks in the Tiffany Archives contain numerous studies for the scene, like the one above left, undoubtedly based on illustrations of Native American life by George Catlin and Alfred Jacob Miller. The sharp-shooting match on September 18, 1879 was again won by the New York team, and Major General Hancock presented the trophy at the N.R.A.'s meeting on the evening of September 20 at the State Arsenal in New York. At some point after 1955 the oak and laurel branches and the eagle disappeared, and the surviving pieces were mounted on a board with a smaller replacement of the original eagle. It now belongs to the Civilian Marksmanship Program, which hopes to restore it to its original condition. ✍

Table centerpiece shown at the 1876 Centennial Exhibition in Philadelphia; the swan's body was filled with fruit when the centerpiece was in use. The *National Repository* commented, "It is treated, of course in a very conventional [i.e., stylized] manner; very richly ornamented in the profuse manner of the Orientals. The feathers are wrought by the *repoussé* process . . . and the trappings on the breast are separately made and applied by heat." (July 1878)

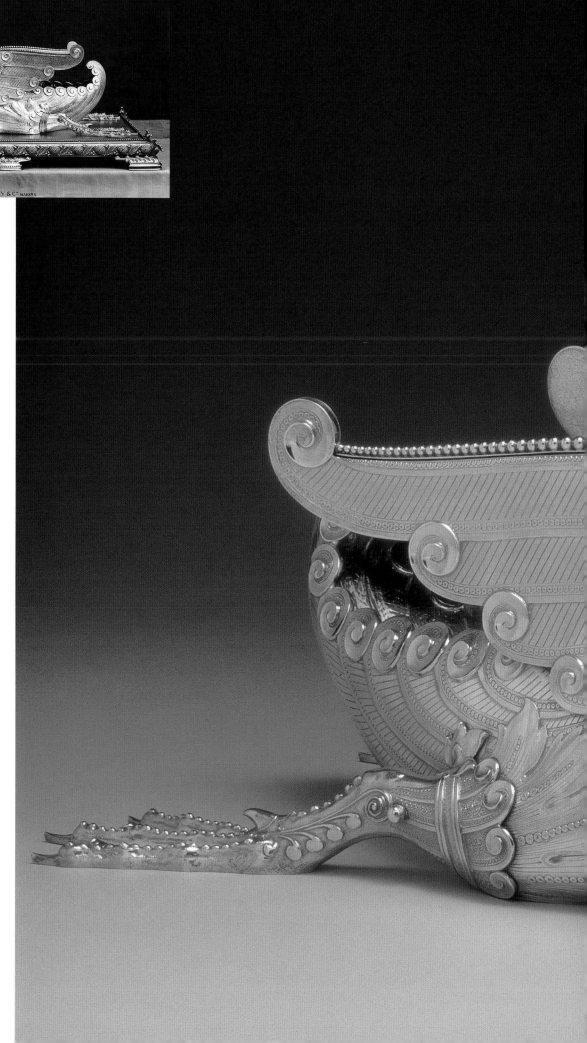

☞ Tiffany's 1876 photograph showing an artistic arrangement of silver displayed at the Centennial Exhibition in Philadelphia, including Eugene J. Soligny's Henri II style salver at left, one of James Gordon Bennett's candelabra featuring Native American warriors at center (see page 113), three Japanesque vases, one Japanesque pitcher, and the Saracenic coffeepot illustrated on page 63. The Native American–style salver at upper right is otherwise unknown; it may have been the work of Eugene J. Soligny. ☜

☞ Designed in the Renaissance Revival's so-called Henry II style, this niello-inlaid salver with the Old French legend "Lequel Des Deux Escouteray [which of the two shall I listen to?]" depicting a young woman listening to cupids at each of her ears has curious Oriental echoes in its design. The woman seems to be modeled more on an Indian Hindu goddess than on a lady of the court of Henri II and Catherine de Medici. It was most likely designed by Eugene J. Soligny for the 1876 Centennial Exposition in Philadelphia in response to his mentor Léonard Morel-Ladeuil's plaque, "Pompeian Lady at her Toilet," in the Elkington display at the Philadelphia Exhibition. Tiffany's displayed this salver again at the 1878 Paris Exposition. ☜

☞ Wall plaque signed by Eugene J. Soligny. The silver center has a repoussé-chased personification of Night. The damascened iron border has silver maple leaves and gold seedpods, and the rim is copper. The plaque has a French import control mark, and it may have been one of four allegorical plates designed by Soligny shown at the 1878 Paris Exposition. ☜

Wine jug in the form of a pig annoyed by a dragonfly. Animal-form wine jugs were popular in nineteenth-century England, and this could have been designed and chased circa 1890 by Eugene J. Soligny, whose sketchbooks eloquently illustrate his love of satire.

Designed by James H. Whitehouse and chased by Eugene J. Soligny, this testimonial vase in the form of an Army canteen was made for the cartoonist Thomas Nast (see page 84) pursuant to a subscription fund sponsored by *The Army and Navy Journal*. The bas-relief on the front, which is entirely Soligny's work and is signed with his initials, was described by *Harper's Weekly:* "The principle [sic] interest . . . both artistically and otherwise, centres in the splendid repoussé picture representing THOMAS NAST receiving a decoration from the Goddess of Liberty in the presence of the army of the United States. The details of this design are beautifully carried out, the perspective showing the long line of troops and distant glistening bayonets, while in the foreground stand the star-crowned goddess and the artist whom the army has honored." (February 15, 1879) The back is inscribed, "Presented to Thomas Nast by his friends in the Army and Navy of the United States in recognition of the patriotic use he has made of his rare abilities as the artist of the people. The gift of 3,500 officers and enlisted men of the Army and Navy of the United States." Many Americans were objecting to maintaining a high level of military spending in peacetime, but Nast—and the readers of *The Army and Navy Journal*—thought otherwise. When he accepted the testimonial on February 1, 1879, Nast said, "I honor the Army and the Navy. I honor them for their gallantry during the war and their useful services in peace, for the Army and the Navy of the United States I regard as a kind of university, a reservoir of knowledge, a school of manners. Other departments of the Government have been corrupt, but the Army and the Navy have kept their honor untarnished in the worst perils of our country, and they constitute to-day an unanswerable argument for permanency, and for just such a system of promotion in the civil service." (*The New York Times*, February 2, 1879) ABOVE RIGHT: A study for the Nast vase from Soligny's sketchbook.

On September 2, 1884 a group of eighteen Minneapolis businessmen, including flour magnate Charles A. Pillsbury, presented this 34-inch-long plaque or tray to "Empire Builder" James J. Hill (1838–1916), who was then president of the St. Paul and Pacific Railroad. These men were commemorating the railroad's completing a 2,100-foot-long stone bridge across the Mississippi River linking Minneapolis with St. Paul. The etched central image shows the bridge, and reliefs in the border depict scenes from Hill's life: a bison hunt, a dogsled, Hill assisting the driver of a broken cart, shipping on the Mississippi River, Hill's former steamboat the *Selkirk*, Hill's farm, and the Angus, Shorthorn, and Jersey cattle that Hill had introduced to the Midwest. Hill's portrait medallion at top center was chased by Eugene J. Soligny.

A pair of "Birds and Branches" silver-gilt compotes dating from about 1884. This elaborately conceived design must be the work of Eugene J. Soligny, with probable inspiration for the configurations of ferns and leaves from Charles Grosjean's elaborate "American Flora" tea and coffee service made for Mary Jane Morgan in the early 1880s (see page 146).

Japanesque ice bowl, 11 inches in diameter, made in 1877.
Two cast walruses and ice floes rest upon the cross-shaped base.
The stem has a gilt band, and the bowl has applied partly gilt pine-
cones and pine branches. Eugene J. Soligny's drawings of walruses
in his sketchbook at the Tiffany Archives strongly suggest that he
modeled these castings, which were used on a number of other pieces.
INSET: Soligny's study for the walrus figures. ◥

CHARLES T. GROSJEAN

uring a short but brilliant career of less than twenty years at Tiffany & Co., Charles T. Grosjean created one of Tiffany's most enduring designs, "Chrysanthemum," as well as two of its other most distinguished flatsilver patterns, "Lap over Edge" and "Wave Edge."

He has also recently been generally credited with a major role in the design of the intricate and massive Mackay dinner and dessert service, which drew great attention to Tiffany & Co.'s superiority in silversmithing at the Paris Exposition of 1878. In 1884–85, he contributed to Tiffany's tradition of silver based on Native American life and costume with a series of flatsilver pieces with sculpted, figural finials based on George Catlin's depictions of the ritualistic dances of American Indians.

Grosjean (1841–1888) came from a silversmithing family. His father, Charles Sr. or "Carl" (1814–1865), was a silversmith from Württemberg who came to New York in 1836 and from there moved to Boston in 1845, where he was in partnership with silversmith John H. Woodward (b.1817, Massachusetts), of whom little is known. Their firm, founded in Boston in 1847 as Woodward and Grosjean (located at 13 Court Square) moved to New York five years later, when, as Grosjean and Woodward, it found a location near Tiffany's at 77 Duane Street. From 1857 until 1862, when the firm was dissolved, they were established at 203 Centre Street, almost next door to John C. Moore and Edward C. Moore's shop at 207 Centre Street. Charles Grosjean, Sr., supplied Tiffany & Co. with silverware from the early 1850s until his untimely death from consumption.

Grosjean and Woodward's most popular products were their baluster-form tea and coffee sets draped with elaborately chased flowers, scrolling leaves, birds, ivy, or chinoiserie. They typically had finely cast "rustic" Rococo Revival spouts and handles; domed covers chased with flutes; and accompanying water pitchers with graceful cast leaf-form spouts. Tiffany's sold many versions of these sets during the 1850s, as did other New York and Boston jewelers and even Hayden & Whilden in far-off Charleston, South Carolina. The mixed inspirations from eighteenth-century German porcelain and

Teapot with repoussé-chased Chinese figures, buildings, and trees; its style reflects the mid-nineteenth-century revival of eighteenth-century chinoiserie. Part of the earliest known Tiffany's tea set, it was made circa 1853 by Grosjean & Woodward for Tiffany, Young & Ellis, the predecessor of Tiffany & Co. The tea set bears a resemblance to the chinoiserie of eighteenth-century German porcelain, and it may have been designed by Gustave Herter, who later became America's leading furniture designer. (Herter emigrated from Germany to New York in 1848 and was said to have worked for Tiffany's, but none of his Tiffany designs is documented.) The forms of this tea set were popular models: Grosjean & Woodward made many similar tea sets for Tiffany's and for other American retailers, but only one other extant example has similar chinoiserie motifs. Tea sets of closely related design were made by at least two other manufacturers: Jones, Ball & Co. in Boston, and the Gorham Co. in Providence; Gorham displayed a very similar tea set at the 1851 Rhode Island State Fair.

⚞ Centerpiece with bear-head handles, probably designed by Charles T. Grosjean circa 1870. The 9½-inch-diameter bowl is chased with water lilies and a narcissus, the foot with berries and stylized leaves. ⚟

silver design gave these essentially Rococo sets an unusual flavor amongst the more English- or French-inspired designs of other American silversmiths.

After the senior Grosjean's death in 1865, Charles T. Grosjean took over the silver business, but, at only twenty-four, was apparently unable to successfully manage it, and the remaining assets were sold in 1866 to a New York silversmith of Dutch descent, William Bogert. The young Charles T. Grosjean then worked for William Bogert & Co., which supplied their often ornate, slightly Elkingtonesque (or, more accurately, Wilhelm the First German Neo-Classic Revival style) silverware exclusively to Tiffany & Co. until Tiffany & Co., after buying out Edward C. Moore's interest in their Prince Street silverworks in 1868, stopped orders to Bogert soon after in 1869. (It is worth noting that William Bogert's partner and chief designer, Bernard D. Biederhase [d. 1874], was German, with strong ties to other German silversmiths working in New York, which may account for the weighty Germanic look of Bogert & Co.'s silverwares, if not for its imitations of Tiffany designs. He was sued on two occasions by Tiffany & Co. for patent

infringements.) As previously noted, Charles T. Grosjean and James H. Whitehouse's younger brother, Frederick, both of whom worked for Bogert, would leave to join Tiffany's in 1869. As a result of this, echoes of the Bogert style of silver on cast plinths with neoclassic feet, often incongruously combined with handles bearing the cast and sculpted heads of American wildlife, would appear at Tiffany's about 1870. American elk- and bear-head handles had, of course, been a feature of Moore's silver since the 1850s; however, the combination of bear-head handles with Hercules mask feet or bear heads on a centerpiece bowl chased with water lilies and narcissus suggests the hand of ex-Bogert silversmiths at Tiffany & Co.

The credit often given to Charles T. Grosjean as principal "designer" of the magnificent 1,250-piece Mackay service of 1877–78 is based on a mistranslation published in an obscure article in the *Pittsburgh Evening and Weekly Chronicle* on August 6, 1878, quoting from the July 24, 1878, issue of New York's French newspaper, the *Courrier des Etats-Unis.* The original French text states that Mr. Grosjean had orchestrated or put together (*"composé"*) the Mackay silver, not that he had designed (*"dessiné"*) it, and that two other Tiffany & Co. workmen, Isidore Heydet, a sculptor, and Henry Friebel

“Chrysanthemum” pattern after-dinner coffee service and water pitcher covered with repoussé-chased foliage populated with wood spirits dancing and playing musical instruments. The feet are decorated with chrysanthemums. Designed by Charles T. Grosjean circa 1880–85.

A pair of 21½-inch-tall eight-light candelabra with applied chrysanthemums and leaves probably designed by Charles T. Grosjean, who patented Tiffany's "Chrysanthemum" flatware pattern in 1880; it is still in production. The candelabra were given to Caroline C. ("Daisy") Beard upon her marriage to John H. Schults, Jr. on December 3, 1890. This marriage united the families of two remarkably successful Brooklyn businessmen. Daisy's father, William Beard, emigrated from Ireland in 1835, prospered in street and railroad construction, then developed the Erie Basin on the Brooklyn waterfront. John's father, the German-born John H. Shults, Sr., was the proprietor of one of the largest bakeries in the world—producing 300,000 loaves of bread per day—and a noted trotting horse owner. The wedding took place at Daisy's widowed mother's house at 140 Amity Street, and *The Brooklyn Daily Eagle*'s account took note of the wedding presents: "From Mr. Shults' father came a check for a quarter of a million dollars. . . . Quite the most beautiful present in the whole collection was a solid silver dinner service of thirty pieces including a magnificent candelabra. Other presents were a set of twelve solid silver finger bowls, which were exhibited at the Paris Exposition; a fancy center table with Sèvres ornamentations, bronze and marble statuary, exquisite paintings, costly china and silverware, and an endless variety of miscellaneous mementos, all costly and beautiful. It is doubtful if a more magnificent display of presents has ever been seen in Brooklyn." (December 4, 1890)

One of a pair of 30¼-inch-tall fifteen-light candelabra decorated with acanthus. Tiffany's ledger reads, "Candelabra . . . Vanderbilt . . . Each 1400.00 D. cost." (It also states that they each have twenty lights.) They were almost certainly made circa 1883 for either Cornelius Vanderbilt or his brother William K. Vanderbilt. These young men were the principal heirs to their grandfather and father's New York Central railroad fortune; both built grand houses on Fifth Avenue in 1881–83 (Cornelius at the northwest corner of 57th Street, William at the northwest corner of 52nd Street), and both commissioned custom-designed flatware from Tiffany's. Custom-designed flatware was exceedingly expensive because it required new designs and new hand-made dies: Tiffany's made only six custom flatware services in the nineteenth century, all for famously extravagant clients. The Vanderbilts' flatware services were designed by Charles T. Grosjean, and it is likely that he designed these candelabra as well. They sold at Sotheby's on January 21, 1996, for $96,000.

("Friebel" too is incorrect; his name was "Triebel"), led the team of some forty "French, English and German" silver chasers that labored two years to produce its lavish floral decorations. The same article uses the same word *composé* to describe the well-known sculptor and die-sinker F. Antoine Heller's role in the orchestration of Edward C. Moore's "Olympian" pattern (patented under Moore's name on August 12, 1879, but introduced at the Paris Exposition of 1878.)

The argument for Grosjean's role in the creation of the Mackay service is somewhat reinforced by his obituary (*New York Tribune*, March 6, 1888) which cites his "specimens of art silverware exhibited by Tiffany & Co. at the Paris Exposition of 1878, for which the firm obtained the prize medal." However, the range of "art silverware" sent by Tiffany & Co. to the Paris Exposition of 1878 was panoramic, from Edward C. Moore's great Japanesque wares, to the mixed "Indian"-Orientalist style Mackay service, to Whitehouse's Bryant Vase, and on to the so-called Native American style of the Bennett candelabrum. The medal was for all, collectively.

James H. Whitehouse was Tiffany's resident expert on heraldry, and there can be little doubt that he designed Mrs. Mackay's Hungerford family coat of arms for the occasion. These arms appear prominently throughout the service.

The flatsilver for the Mackay service was incontestably designed by Edward C. Moore, who was issued U.S. Patent No. 10524 on it, March 12, 1878. Moore is credited by the noted Tiffany silver scholar Charles H. Carpenter, Jr., in his 1997 book *Tiffany Silver:* "The flower-encrusted design has its origin in Persia and Mogul India. In fact, Tiffany called the design of the whole service *Indian*. Unquestionably, Edward C. Moore, who supervised the design of the service, was influenced by the dense overall designs of the Near Eastern metal works in his own collection. But he did not copy the designs. His designs are not flat like their prototypes. They are more three dimensional, more sculptural, and far more varied in their ornamentation. The repoussé chasing is . . . architectural, . . . ordered. The formal elements of the pieces come through with clarity."

There is, as Carpenter points out, no reason to doubt that the overall concept for the Mackay service design was Edward C. Moore's; but there is no reason to doubt either that Grosjean's participation was of great importance. The much admired tête-a-tête set from the service is a natural evolution of the repoussé-chased baluster-form tea and coffee services

Ice cream serving bowl, 14 inches in diameter, with an Islamic floral band around the body and four handles with peacocks on perches. Its style is similar to a service with elephant handles made in 1876, and the festoon and spirals on the feet are similar to those on the breast of the swan centerpiece shown at the 1876 Philadelphia Exhibition (see pages 130–31). Made under Edward C. Moore's direction, it is a stylistic predecessor of the 1878 Mackay service, and like the Mackay service is probably the work of several Tiffany designers—such as Charles T. Grosjean, James H. Whitehouse, Eugene J. Soligny, and others—working together. Tiffany's made several identical or very similar ice cream bowls.

Archival photo of a Saracenic ice cream bowl designed by Edward C. Moore, Charles Grojean, and others circa 1876–78. Similar handles were used on the hot-water kettle of the "American Flora" tea and coffee service made for Mary Jane Morgan circa 1884 (see page146).

Tea and coffee service made for the 1876 Centennial Exhibition in Philadelphia. Tiffany's catalogue listed as, "Tea Service in the Persian style, elaborately adorned with flowers, executed entirely by the repoussé process." *The Jewelers' Circular and Horological Review* reported, "The most wonderful specimen of repoussé work [in Tiffany's] exhibit, is a tea set of five pieces; Persian in outline, with the flowers and foliage so beautifully brought out, that a botanist could classify every leaf and flower." (July 9, 1876) This set, or another very much like it, was on sale at Tiffany's New York store in December 1876, when *The Daily Graphic* reported, "One tea-set of five pieces occupied a man one whole year. It is in elaborate Persian designs, leaves and flowers overlaying each other; and when it is considered that this delicacy of flower and foliage is obtained by beating up the plain surface through slow hand labor, the price, $3,000, is no longer a marvel; in fact it seems very cheap." (December 11, 1876)

of Grosjean and Woodward of the 1850s, still Rococo Revivalist in feeling but with greater freedom and vigor to its floral patterns and with greater lavishness and virtuosity in the high relief repoussé chasing. This set must be Grosjean's.

Other pieces, such as the punch bowl, the ice cream dish, and the bottle sleigh—with their curious combinations of grape vines and forget-me-nots with elephant trunks, or the sleigh's stylized lily-of-the-valley motifs combined with a fig tree—are in line with Grosjean's eclectic earlier work. However, what Carpenter refers to as the "architectural, . . . ordered" nature of the overall designs and the "clarity" imposed by the formal elements of those designs would most likely be the result of the collaboration of Edward C. Moore's unequaled Orientalist design vocabulary and James H. Whitehouse's formal-to-severe sense of architectural order. There is, again, nothing in Grosjean's work before or after that would justify crediting him with the entire design of the Mackay service. The overall credit, if not credit for many of its parts, surely belongs to Edward C. Moore.

In 1878 Grosjean originated his best-known design, "Chrysanthemum," with its radiant flowering heads and undulating leaves. Photographs in the Tiffany Archives indicate that a serving spoon and a pair of sauceboats were shown at the Paris Exposition of 1878, and that Grosjean was granted U.S. Patent No. 11968 on September 21, 1880. The hollowware he designed for "Chrysanthemum" had forms that Tiffany's journals term "Apple Shape." They are, as Carpenter accurately describes them in *Tiffany Silver*, "traditional baroque shapes with squat, apple-shaped bodies. Incised lines form

LEFT:

⌁ Archival photograph of a coffeepot, tray, and sugar bowl in the Saracenic style made for the 1878 Paris Exposition. Closely related to the Mackay service—and made at the same time—the design of these pieces can be attributed to James H. Whitehouse and Charles T. Grosjean working under the direction of Edward C. Moore. The border of the tray has Chinese clouds that repeat Moore's enameling pattern of storks on page 25. ⌁

reeding at the corners of the pieces, leaving the rounded, swelling parts of the body unadorned." Far from the strong lines, the robust forms, and the formality of the Mackay service, to its great credit, the fluid reversing curves of the undulating leaf patterns of "Chrysanthemum" give it a proto-Art Nouveau stylishness altogether lacking in its peculiarly proportioned forms.

Some pieces of "Chrysanthemum" hollowware made about 1881 were completely covered with repoussé-chased, heavy, scrolling foliage strangely populated by bacchic scenes of putti dancing or playing ancient musical instruments whose echoes of the German Rococo Revival unavoidably suggest Grosjean as their author. If that is the case, it is inconceivable that he could have designed the Mackay service without major help from Moore, Whitehouse, and others including Soligny, who alone at Tiffany's had the peculiar bent to his imagination to have conjured up the service's elephant-trunk feet.

Grosjean's final well-known work is the intriguing series of flatware pieces with cast figures based on George Catlin's depictions of Indian dances. These were first executed in 1884 and patented in 1885, but are far from Tiffany's first use of Catlin's work, as evidenced by the previous comments on the Native American figures of Eugene Soligny. Even before Soligny, about 1850 John C. Moore had made a twenty-inch-long silver relief plaque for Tiffany, Young & Ellis depicting a grisly coming-of-age torture ceremony of the Mandan tribe of the upper Missouri River Valley that was based on an 1832 painting by Catlin.

ABOVE:

Saracenic tea set made from a design stamped July 29, 1887. Its basic shapes are those of the "Persian" tea set made for the 1876 Philadelphia Exhibition (see page 145), while its decor is of the family of Edward C. Moore's lavish and fluid Saracenic pieces shown at the 1889 Paris Exposition.

OPPOSITE:

Monumental hot-water kettle on stand, part of the "American Flora" tea and coffee service made for Mary Jane Morgan and repurchased by Tiffany's at the auction of her silver on March 10, 1886 for $3,400. Tiffany's sold the Morgan service with the salver illustrated on page 159 for a price variously reported as $10,000 and $12,000 to the Chicago art collector Mrs. Potter Palmer, who loaned the ensemble to Tiffany's for display at the 1889 Paris Exposition. The kettle's handle is similar to the handles on the ice cream bowl shown at the bottom of page 144.

Grosjean's health failed during the winter of 1887–88, possibly as a result of the strain of severe labor disputes and a silver chasers' strike at Tiffany's Prince Street works from March to June of 1887. Exhausted from overwork, and possibly demoralized by his co-workers' total capitulation to management at the end of the labor disputes, he was advised by his doctors to find a change of climate and complete relaxation. He left New York for Bermuda, but too late.

His death, like his father's, was premature and was noted in the *Jewelers' Circular* of April 1888: "Charles T. Grosjean . . . was forty-seven years of age, and learned the silvesmith's trade with his father, of the late firm of Grosjean & Woodward. He soon made his mark and became very adept in his art. He was admitted into his father's firm, and about twenty years ago was offered a position with Tiffany & Co., as superintendent of the silverware branch of their business. He was very devoted to his art, in which he achieved distinction, being spoken of as one of the best living decorators of silver. He overworked himself, however, and when his physician got him to consent to go to Bermuda it was already too late and he died two days after landing there."

In 1873 John W. Mackay (pronounced "Mackie") and his partners discovered the "Big Bonanza" in Virginia City, Nevada, said to be the most profitable gold and silver vein in history. Not long thereafter Mackay's wife, the former Marie Louise Hungerford, on a visit to the mine with her husband, asked him for enough silver to make a proper dinner service. He complied, eventually shipping over half a ton of silver to Tiffany's Prince Street factory. Made in 1877–78, the Mackays' 1,250-piece "Dinner and Dessert Service for Twenty-four Persons" was one of the wonders of the Gilded Age. Designed under the supervision of Edward C. Moore with significant design contributions by Charles T. Grosjean and lesser contributions by James H. Whitehouse and others, its heavy floral ornamentation is in the "Indian" style. Each piece bears Mrs. Mackay's "MLM" monogram and the Hungerford coat of arms, redesigned by Whitehouse for this service. The custom-designed flatware was patented by Moore on March 12, 1878. When the service was completed, Tiffany's shipped it in nine specially-fitted plush-lined wooden boxes to the 1878 Paris Exposition; it took four men to carry each box. Richard Whiteing wrote in the *New York World,* "It is an ingenious device of [Mr. Mackay's] for getting rid of his ever-growing load from his silver mine. The costly dross, I suppose, was lumbering up his cellars, and so he sent a ton of it to Tiffany to be worked up in a form which would admit of its storage on the sideboard. Tiffany has done its best, and of course the service is a wonder. I cannot say that it is simple, but it is everything else. . . . One spoon differeth wholly from another spoon in the glory of its chasers work; nay one section of dish or dish-cover differeth from the other. Each piece bears a shield, a motto: 'And God my support,' in the French tongue—and a coronet with strawberry leaves, which would seem to show that in the remote past some member of the family was a duke. Why not? Many a duke would be proud to be what the family is now. I, however, would be content to drop dukedoms and such trash if I owned the largest share in the Consolidated Virginia Mine, but that is a only the confession of an individual weakness. Mr. Mackay, would, no doubt, do the same, only he feels it a duty not to be ashamed of his poor dead kin. I regard this coronet on the service, then, as a visible symbol of lowliness of origin, set there as a safeguard against pride, and bow before it accordingly, whenever I see one of the spoons." (July 11, 1878) After showing it at the exposition, Tiffany's delivered the service to the Mackays' sumptuous new apartment in Paris. ✍

Mary Jane Morgan, widow of railroad and shipping magnate Charles Morgan, commissioned this pair of enormous (70¼-inch-tall) twenty-light candelabra on torchère stands in the Italian Renaissance style in 1884. The bases are decorated with poppy seed-pods and swirling chrysanthemums, the vase-shaped stems have applied female caryatids and trophies, and the globes under the candle stems boast applied poppies and acanthus leaves. The candelabra were part of a vast collection of rare orchid plants, French academic and Barbizon School paintings, Oriental porcelain, and Tiffany silver that Mrs. Morgan displayed in her New York house at 7 East Twenty-sixth Street. She died suddenly on July 5, 1885; her orchids were auctioned in October and the balance of her collection over six days the following March by the American Art Association, the predecessor of Sotheby's New York. A *New York Times* editorial commented chivalrously, "while she spent in a princely fashion there was far less recklessness in her outlays than she has been somewhat hastily charged with in some quarters." (February 11, 1886) Bidders at the Morgan silver sale on March 10 included Charles Crocker of San Francisco, John T. Martin of Brooklyn, and Edward C. Moore's friend Samuel P. Avery, the leading art dealer in New York. The *Herald* reported that the candelabra were sold for $8,100 to "the representative of Howard & Co., presumably on an order. The two are said to have cost Mrs. Morgan $24,000!" (March 11, 1886) *The Jewelers' Circular and Horological Review* commented, "Such a wealth of rich goods being thrown on the market all at once, it was hardly to be expected that full prices would be offered for them." (April 1886) The candelabra eventually passed to the Kimbell Art Foundation in Fort Worth, Texas, which sold them at Sotheby's on June 24, 1987 for $440,000.

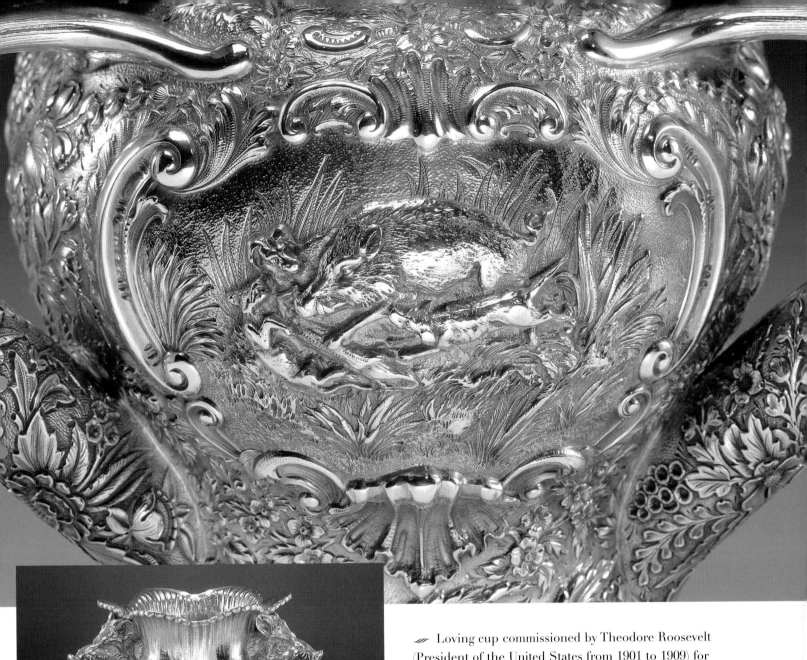

Loving cup commissioned by Theodore Roosevelt (President of the United States from 1901 to 1909) for presentation to the Porcellian Club in 1880, when he was a twenty-two-year-old senior at Harvard College and the club's undergraduate vice president. Founded at Harvard in 1791 as a banqueting organization, the club's name was derived from the Latin diminutive for "pig" and refers to its favorite dish, roast pork. The club's symbol, a boar's head, is represented by boars' heads atop the cup's three handles and serving as its three feet. The cartouche (like the boar's heads, undoubtedly designed and made by Eugene J. Soligny) shows three dogs attacking a boar at the climax of a hunt, and there are *cors de chasse* (French hunting horns) under the medallions on each of the three sides. The body and handles of the 10½-inch-tall cup are covered with repoussé-chased flowers (probably designed by Charles Grosjean) similar to the flowers on the tea and coffee service made for Mary Jane Morgan (see page 146), and its fluted lip is characteristic of Charles Osborne's work. Like the Mackay service and many presentation pieces of the time, this cup was a collaboration among several designers; the quality of its chasing demonstrates Soligny's unparalleled craftsmanship. ❧

CHAPTER 3:
THE FLOWERING OF AN AMERICAN STYLE

CHARLES OSBORNE

JOHN T. CURRAN

PAULDING FARNHAM

Ashbel P. Fitch was a successful New York lawyer and financier. He was first elected to Congress from Harlem in 1886 as a Republican, but on May 10, 1888, he made a widely-publicized speech attacking the high tariff policy advocated by Republican congressman (and future President) William McKinley. Backed by Richard Croker of Tammany Hall (see page 109), Fitch switched parties and won reelection on the Democratic ticket in November 1888. In 1890, despite the passage of the McKinley Tariff in April, he again won reelection by a majority of 16,000 votes. Anonymous citizens of Harlem presented him with this punch bowl at a ceremony on April 8, 1891 at the Harlem Democratic Club. The large inscription inside the bowl reads, "Presented to Ashbel P. Fitch by friends in the Thirteenth District in commemoration of his third election to Congress, November, 1890, by the largest majority ever given in New-York to a candidate for that office, and in recognition of his distinguished services for Tariff Reform, in defence [sic] of the rights of the City of New York and in the cause of pure and impartial government for the People of the United States of America. Harlem, April 8th, 1891." The bowl, 22 inches in diameter, was probably designed by Charles Osborne and was made from a hammering, mounting, and etching design stamped August 10, 1881. It is repoussé-chased with swirling water and has nine applied mermaids supporting the rim. The aquatic imagery suggests that it may have been originally intended as a yachting trophy.

One of the most intriguing, and most elusive, figures in the history of Tiffany silver design is Charles Osborne, a brilliant designer whose work is generally associated with the silver of the Whiting Manufacturing Company, where he was head designer both before and after his nine-year sojourn at Tiffany & Co. (January 1879–December 1887).

Osborne was born in England on September 21, 1847 (d. New York, March 23, 1920) and brought to America by his parents David and Ann Webb Osborne in 1855 or 1856. He studied at New York's National Academy of Design and then in 1871, at age twenty-three, became Whiting's chief designer in North Attleboro, Massachusetts. His designs were distinguished from the start, and in 1874 he competed with James H. Whitehouse of Tiffany & Co. for the design of the Bryant Vase.

In 1875 Whiting's North Attleboro plant was ravaged by a fire, and whatever could be salvaged was moved to a new location in New York. Back in New York, Osborne became

Japanesque pitcher designed by Charles Osborne circa 1880. An eccentric piece; the hexagonal hand-hammering pattern is highly unusual, and although embellishing it with repoussé spirals required virtuoso hammering and chasing where the patterns meet, their juxtaposition seems forced. The painstakingly accurate lobster climbing up the side is almost surrealistic.

acquainted with Edward C. Moore, whose work he greatly admired, and the stylistic evidence of several pieces of Japanesque silver shown by Tiffany's in Paris in 1878 suggests that Moore had begun to commission designs from Osborne as early as 1877. Then, following the triumph of Tiffany's silverware at the Paris Exposition of 1878, Osborne decided to leave Whiting. His resignation letter of November 15, 1878 (now in the Osborne Collection at Winterthur) stated:

> I have long felt that I was making no real progress in my art work; and that I would be glad if I could find an opening, a place, where I could have a larger field for what talent I do possess. I felt that what I knew was superficial and that I needed to go to school—for many things were to be learned that I was not in the way of learning—that I needed more solid basis in my art education and that I should properly be under a master—who could guide and instruct me so as to make me more able & thorough for the rest of my life. I became acquainted with Mr. Moore of Tiffany & Co. and recognized in him a man whom I believe has in him all the qualities I desire in a master. I broached the subject to him, and explained my wishes. He has been good enough to think favorable on the matter— and the result is that I have found an engagement with him for a period of three years. I could have gone from you to other places—but would not. I feel however That I cannot afford to let this opportunity for higher development pass by."

Immediately after Charles Osborne's arrival at Tiffany's silverworks in January 1879, his hand becomes recognizable in the many Japanesque silver designs he collaborated on with Edward C. Moore. The spiral, a device usually foreign to the work of Moore as well as to that of Whitehouse, Soligny, or Grosjean, suddenly appears as both a dominant formal element of decoration and as structure of overall form and design.

During Osborne's sojourn at Tiffany's, this spiraling of line, pattern, and form took on greater and greater importance, manifesting itself as a dominant motif in much of Tiffany's post–Exposition of 1878 Japanesque silver, in its chased floral ornamentations, and finally in its Saracenic enameled showpieces of the 1880s.

Comparisons of floral and Orientalist motifs on Whiting silver of the end of the 1870s with Tiffany silver of the beginning

Parcel-gilt punch bowl 17 inches in diameter, one of two trophies contributed by Elisha A. Buck, proprietor of *The Spirit of the Times,* for winners of schooner and sloop races held off New Bedford, Massachusetts, during the 1881 cruise of the New York Yacht Club, when its members competed against the Eastern Yacht Club's members. This trophy was won by the schooner *Halcyon,* owned by General Charles J. Paine, a prominent Bostonian who was a member of both clubs. Charles H. Carpenter, Jr., commented, "It is certainly one of the most remarkable pieces of silver made in the nineteenth century. It has great architectural strength and unity, for the water bug and the crab applied to the base, and the deeply chased tendrils climbing up the stem, and the applied dolphins around the rim are all in perfect scale with the bowl and eminently in keeping with its hand-hammered surface. The form is conventional and functional, but this is a far cry from the usual silver punch bowl of the time. It is pure sculpture. The motifs did have their origins in Japanese art, but the bowl is not really Japanese in feeling. The designer [probably Charles Osborne under Edward C. Moore's direction] and the silversmith have created a completely new style. ("Nineteenth-century silver in the New York Yacht Club," *Antiques,* September 1977) The circle of overlapping dolphins around the lip may have inspired John T. Curran's design for the Tarpon Vase shown at the 1893 Chicago Exposition (see page 189). A nearly identical trophy—with a grappling iron and rope instead of Japanesque sea creatures on its base—was won by Daniel Cook's *Tidal Wave,* most likely in the First Class centerboard schooner race in the New York Yacht Club's regatta on June 16, 1881. The *Tidal Wave* trophy sold for $129,000 at Sotheby's New York on January 20, 1998.

of the 1880s point inevitably to the conclusion that this new and eventually influential hand in Tiffany silver design was Osborne's.

Suddenly there is a fluidity and sensuality to the chased overall floral patterns quite absent in the flowers of the great Mackay service of 1877–78, but already suggested in Osborne's earlier and intensely floral Whiting silver. These fluid, sensual flowers begin to appear on Edward C. Moore's Japanesque gourd-shaped coffeepots for the first time, and they are clearly Osborne's.

Not long after Osborne's arrival at Tiffany's, at the beginning of December 1880, Edward C. Moore brought a Japanese sword sheath from his private collection to Tiffany's silver design studio to show the designers a Japanese silver chasing method called "pearl chasing," or simply "pearling," by which small round domes or "pearls" are chased into the silver in free-circling, spiraling, or undulating rows, all usually graduated. Soon after, Tiffany's *martelé* Japanesque silverwares begin to display Osborne's spiraling compositions in this new technique. Nautilus shells, starfish, ripe pomegranates exposing their plump seeds, ammonites, the tendrils of vines, and even dancing insects are all adroitly chased in curving graduations of silver "pearls."

The recurring motifs of Osborne's design vocabulary—seashells, seahorses, dolphins, seaweed, mermaids, tritons, and nereids—swim and coil across the surfaces of 1880s Tiffany silver, and the appearances of gracefully chased wild roses, dogwood flowers, and Oriental poppies, which appear to be Osborne signature flowers, are also frequent even on Japanesque *martelé* wares.

In this period, too, there is a collaboration between Tiffany & Co. and the leading English glasshouse of Thomas Webb and Sons, which appears to have its own relation to Osborne. In 1882 Tiffany's had bought from Webb's a neoclassical Renaissance Revival cameo-glass vase called the Pegasus Vase, designed by England's great glass decorator John Northwood. (It is now in the Smithsonian Institution, Washington, D.C.) This began a successful design and business relationship between Webb's and Tiffany's, which would continue throughout the 1880s. Whether Charles Osborne's mother, Ann Webb Osborne, was related to Charles Webb or his brother Thomas Wilkes Webb (whose glasswares had won the grand prize at the Paris Exposition of 1878) is unknown. It is known, however, that the seashell and seaweed patterns of Webb cameo glass retailed by Tiffany's match the seashell and seaweed patterns of Charles Osborne's Tiffany silver. And it is known that Tiffany & Co. sent designs to be executed in cameo glass to Thomas Webb and Sons in Stourbridge, England, and ordered intricately carved models by John Northwood's students, Thomas and George Woodall, the chief cameo glass designers at Webb.

One such piece, a trumpet vase with a geranium motif, was reputedly designed by Mary Jane Morgan, one of Tiffany's most important clients of the early 1880s, for whom a magnificent floral tea and coffee set completed in 1884 and shown at the Paris Exposition of 1889 was created. This extraordinary set's lush and sensual flora, its spirals, and its wild roses all point to Charles Osborne as its author. Could he also have helped Mary Jane Morgan with the geraniums carved on her peach-and-white cameo glass trumpet vase from Webb and Tiffany's? And could he have furnished Webb with the seashell and seaweed motifs on cameo vases retailed by Tiffany's at the same period?

Tiffany silver designs of the 1880s, with their undulating, swirling, and spiraling lines, but also with their curvaceously fleshed out, sensual, and organic forms, have close affinities to the whiplash reverse curve style of Art Nouveau. It stands alone as an easily identifiable personal style of great elegance and virtuosity in the history of Tiffany silver, and it can only be attributed to the genius of Charles Osborne.

Following Osborne's departure from Tiffany & Co. at the end of 1887, strong echoes of this style appear in the work of John T. Curran who, upon the death of Edward C. Moore in 1891, became Tiffany's chief silver designer. It is quite clear that not only Moore but also his close collaborator Osborne were responsible for Curran's education at the Tiffany School. Curran's Art Nouveau-esque silver designs for the World's Columbian Exposition of 1893, including his magnificent Magnolia Vase, are sufficient testimony to this.

Osborne's hand can be seen not only in the 1880s evolution of Tiffany silver's Japanesque and naturalistic floral styles, but in the evolution of Tiffany's and Moore's Saracenic style as well. Here too the spirals, undulations, and reverse curves and the sensual fleshed-out forms take on greater and greater importance leading up to the lush and triumphant collection of chased and enameled Saracenic silverwares shown by Tiffany's at the Paris Exposition of 1889, which

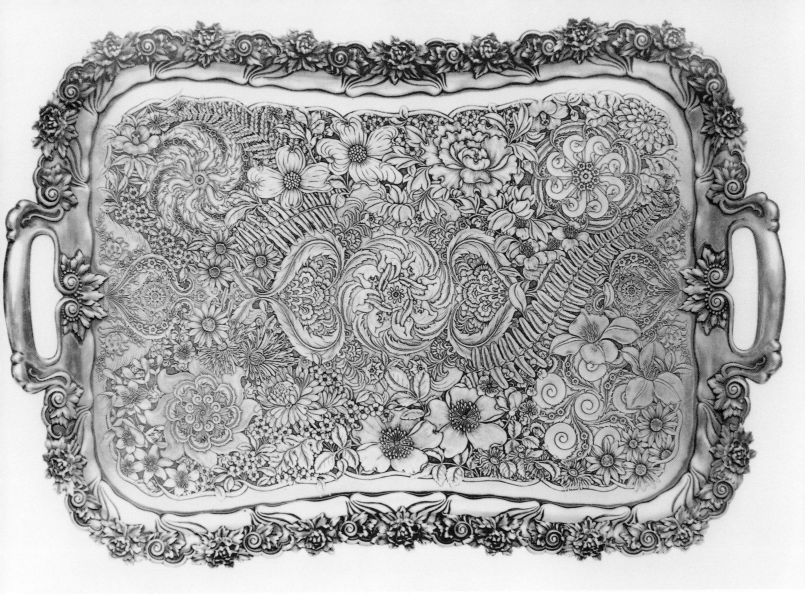

A salver (service tray) designed by Charles Osborne and made between 1879 and 1884. A critic writing in the Spring 1885 issue of *The Connoisseur* praised it in the highest possible terms: "This is a specimen of flat decoration done with the chisel, and finished by tooling. . . the value of the workmanship must be at least twenty times the material. What the collector, in the year 2005 will have to pay for such a specimen, prophesy shrinks from revealing. But it will be a small fortune. At first glance this would strike the eye as being Oriental, perhaps Persian, perhaps North of India in design. But this is from the free use of spiral flat forms, of all others the most useful for flat decoration. These are in the corners, and in the center; and between them is a fairy fantasy of flower forms as deliciously poetic as some of the Shakespearean lines about blossoms. Ferns sweep from corner to centre, and play around the whorls with a grace that is exquisite. Leaves are bent until they are like feathers. Blossoms of the plum tree and of the dogwood, chrysanthemums, sunflowers of the small variety, the pretty petals of myosotis, carnations, peonies, pimpernel, stream from the designer's fingers, and fill up every vacant space, save here and there where one gets a glimpse of a background made black by acids and wrought with tiny spirals. The more one examines this splendid, this crowning effort of the silversmith's art in the nineteenth century, the more one wonders that one could ever have admired the Renaissance and its stupid sequel the Rococo. . . . And all these are natural forms plucked tenderly from the lap of Mother Nature, giving suggestions of garden, and forest, and meadow, and mountain side. They are so mingled, so combined that you do not wonder how they came together. The perfect knowledge of the principles of decoration forbid the thought. Had the artist who conceived this been simply a reproducer of natural forms according to the doctrine of men who preach art without understanding it, there would have been incongruity, grotesqueness and a jarred sense of the mind. Here there is perfection. But not content with the successful treatment of natural forms the artist weds them to Arabesques of the Persian or Indian type. And the result is enchanting, fascinating beyond description." (This critic was a follower of Owen Jones, who advocated flat decoration and Islamic prototypes; Jones's strictures were vehemently opposed by John Ruskin, who advocated the faithful reproduction of nature.) The salver was sold to Mrs. Potter Palmer with the "American Flora" tea and coffee service originally made for Mary Jane Morgan (see page 146).

Copper-on-silver Japanesque chocolate pot designed by Charles Osborne, 10½ inches tall, made in 1879. The sides are repoussé chased, with Osborne's signature spirals, and have applied lobsters. The finial is ivory.

The spiral chasing and hexagonal hand-hammering on the body of this Japanesque vase are typical of Charles Osborne's work; the gourd shape and applied dragonfly are typical of Edward C. Moore's, indicating that they collaborated on its design.

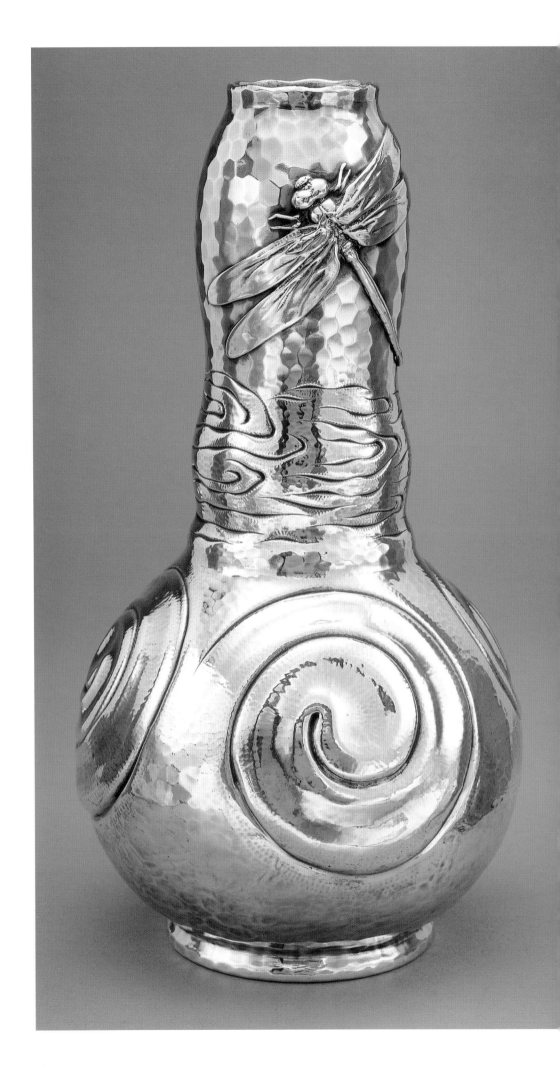

won Tiffany's the grand prize and merited Edward C. Moore the Legion of Honor.

Had Edward C. Moore in the last years of his life so dramatically altered his style to abandon the restrained perfection, grace, and quiet harmony of the great body of his work for a final flourish of lavishness? No, it was Osborne who brought this new voluptuous Orientalist richness to the Saracenic silverwares shown in 1889. (The Tiffany Archives, in fact, have an Osborne drawing for an elaborate Saracenic coffee set bearing the "P" mark of all designs approved to be made for the Paris Exposition of 1889.)

"If Moore is undoubtedly the most famous and best known of all American silverware designers," D. Albert Soeffing writes in his insightful essay "The History of the Origins, Design and Promotion of Tiffany & Co. Holloware" (*Tiffany Retrospective* catalogue, 1999), "Osborne could, arguably, be ranked as second. In large portion, this may be due to the little known circumstances of his employment with Tiffany & Co."

When James Gordon Bennett was again elected commodore of the New York Yacht Club in 1884, he commissioned four Commodore's Cups valued at $500 each for schooner and sloop races sailed off Newport on August 12, 1884. C. Smith Lee's cutter *Oriva* won this Japanesque punch bowl for finishing first in the Second Class Sloop class (single-masted yachts under fifty feet long). The 15⅝-inch-diameter bowl was designed by Charles Osborne; its form is similar to the punch bowl designed by Edward C. Moore that is illustrated on page 42.

Although Charles Osborne is not named as the designer under discussion, an essay entitled "Artistic Silverware" in *The Connoisseur*'s first issue of 1885 accurately extols the virtues of his designs for Tiffany & Co. All of the essay's five illustrations are of Osborne-designed silver.

Discussing the floral waiter (salver) that would be shown in Paris in 1889, The *Connoisseur*'s critic extols the "free use of spiral forms," the ferns that "sweep from corner to centre, and play around the whorls with a grace that is exquisite. The more one examines this splendid, this crowning effort of the silversmith's art in the nineteenth century, the more one wonders that one could ever have admired the Renaissance (Revival) and its stupid sequel the Rococo (Revival). Here there is perfection, but not content with the successful treatment of natural forms, the artist weds them to Arabesques of the Persian or Indian type. And the result is enchanting, is fascinating beyond description."

The author goes on to discuss Osborne's "bendingness" of floral forms, "this airy curving of lines, this trembling delicacy, this fantastic mingling of forms"; his "sweep" of decoration "in harmony with the form of the object"; his "surprising vigor"; his highly decorative use of a "spiral whorl of beaded pearls" to represent an ammonite; or of "scallop shells which join charmingly with seaweed." Finally, the critic notes Osborne's "beautiful line full of incident and interests"; his "exquisite Arabesque fantasies," and "the playfulness that runs through many of his designs."

The essay concludes by paying homage "to the eloquent teachings of the house of Tiffany & Co." by which he means the eloquence of Charles Osborne's designs.

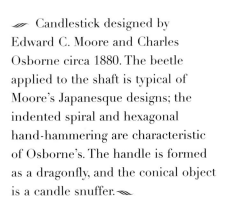

Candlestick designed by Edward C. Moore and Charles Osborne circa 1880. The beetle applied to the shaft is typical of Moore's Japanesque designs; the indented spiral and hexagonal hand-hammering are characteristic of Osborne's. The handle is formed as a dragonfly, and the conical object is a candle snuffer.

Japanesque yachting trophy designed by Charles Osborne, 12¾ inches in diameter. Decorated with seahorses and shells, its feet are similar to those on the cup for schooners won by *Halcyon* in 1882 (opposite). This trophy was won by F. C. Lawrence, Jr.'s *Vixen* for a sloop race sailed in the New York Yacht Club's regatta on June 25, 1883. It sold at Sotheby's for $12,100 on January 30, 1991.

This hand-hammered, parcel-gilt yachting trophy has a water lily on the reverse side (above); the etching of a schooner on the front (below) is rather out of keeping with its Japanesque style. During the New York Yacht Club's 1882 cruise, its members again competed against members of the Eastern Yacht Cub, this time off Marblehead, Massachusetts, on August 14. Presented by the Eastern Yacht Club's flag officers, this trophy was won by General Paine's *Halcyon*, which had won the previous year's schooner race. Another version of this cup—without the schooner and with a frog climbing up the gilt interior—sold for $13,800 at Christie's on June 22, 1994.

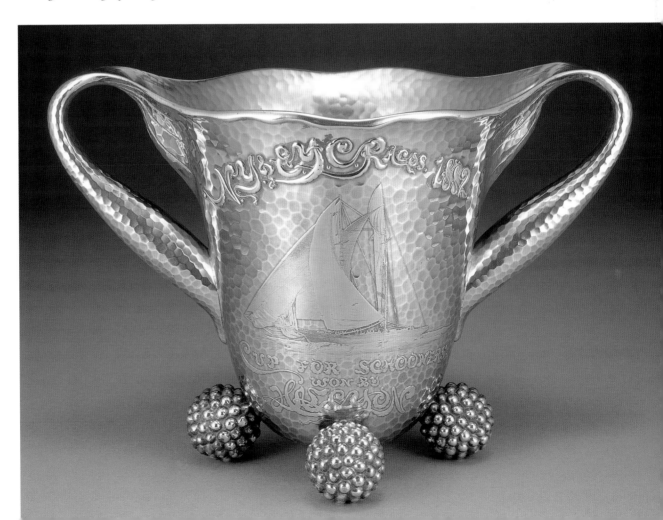

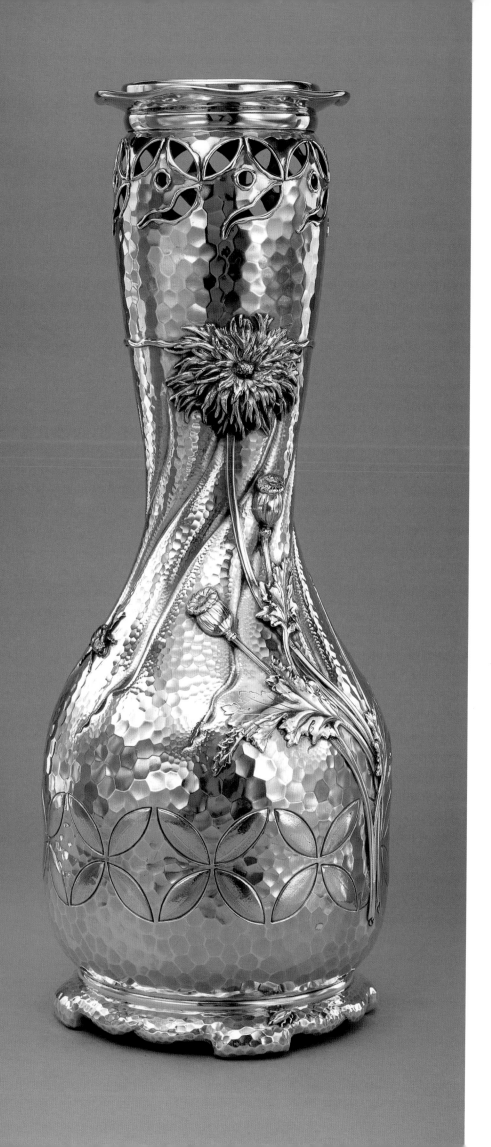

Japanesque vase with an applied chrysanthemum. The sensual flower and spiral fluting indicate that it was probably designed by Charles Osborne circa 1880–85.

OPPOSITE:

A pair of 17½-inch-tall Japanesque candelabra undoubtedly designed by Charles Osborne under the direction of Edward C. Moore and made circa 1881–84; they are listed in Tiffany's pattern book as "Candelabra Gourd Twist." The tops of the gourd-shaped bodies have four twisting vines whose tendrils support the candle holders. The bodies are hand-hammered with hexagons, chased with wisteria vines and crickets, and applied with gilt seedpods. The square bases are chased with spirals and pearling, and applied with bugs and gilt frogs. When the candelabra came up for auction at Christie's on January 21, 2000, the catalogue ascribed them to Edward C. Moore alone, probably due to his extensive (but more restrained) work in the Japanesque style. They sold for $145,500.

OPPOSITE:

Pitcher with repoussé pomegranates and pearling designed by Charles Osborne in 1882. It is 7¾ inches tall. Its affinity with the "tropical pitcher" on page 194 suggests that Osborne's young follower John T. Curran collaborated on the design.

Compote with etched wild roses in the center, 8½ inches in diameter, designed by Charles Osborne and made in 1883. The center and the foot are decorated with half-round beads in a chasing technique called pearling. An often-used feature of Osborne's designs, pearling was invented in 1880 by Edward C. Moore, who told Tiffany's silver chasers to reproduce a motif on a Japanese sword sheath that he brought to the factory on Prince Street.

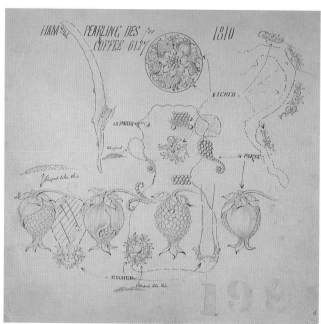

Charles Osborne's circa 1882 pearling design for a Japanesque coffeepot. Osborne probably decided upon the pomegranate motif so that he could use pearling in the design.

Japanesque soup tureen made circa 1885. The divided handles that develop as they descend into the feet, the undulating, indented fringe under the lip, and the placement of the leaves and berries are typical of Charles Osborne's designs.

OPPOSITE:

Japanesque coffeepot. The gourd shape was designed by Edward C. Moore in 1878, and the elaborate floral decoration appears to have been designed by Charles Osborne circa 1884. The pattern is called "sou chow" in Tiffany's pattern book, and its chasing cost was a whopping $800. This pattern was used again on a tea set made for the 1900 Paris Exposition. Tiffany's catalogue listed it, "TEA-SET. Seven pieces and a waiter, richly chased 'sou chow' introducing the more popular American flowers, as follows: chrysanthemum, dog-wood, ragged-sailor, eglantine, marguerites, forget-me-nots, azalias [sic], carnations, heliotropes, butter-cups, marigold, sweet-peas, lily of the valley, pansies, poppy, anemone, meadow beauty, nasturtium, clover, butter-cups [again] and apple-blossom."

Designed by Charles Osborne in the 1880s, the center of this 10½-inch-diameter tray is decorated with roses and ammonites. The spirals of the ammonites and the wavy lines around the rim are pearled. The roses are similar to those on fabrics by the English poet and designer William Morris. Osborne used them frequently in the early 1880s in his designs for Tiffany.

Tea caddy designed by Charles Osborne circa 1882. The stylized wild rose, spirals, and pearling are characteristic of Osborne's work.

Illustration from *The Connoisseur*'s first quarterly issue of 1885 showing a loving cup designed by Charles Osborne. Its description in the accompanying article demonstrates the extent to which Tiffany's silverwares were regarded as important works of art. "Archeologists rave about the repoussé on Macedonian corselets. The time will come when archeologists will rave over this, which is equal in handiwork, and far superior in treatment. Its style is the highest development of naturalism, or the use of natural objects as motives [motifs]. The artist has taken a tulip flower and conventionalized it, but not in any ordinary false acceptation of the term which is to reduce the motive to a conventional form suitable for any decorative purpose. This is the Oriental idea as embodied in arabesque natural forms. He has modified it according to the requirements of the vase, and exigencies and capabilities of repoussé. He has flattened the flower cup, opened the petals, and spread them out like a fan, giving to the edges a beautiful line full of incident and interest. Then by the use of acid he has obtained a sense of color, and with the playfulness that runs though many of his designs he has introduced a wandering bug, a finely executed bit of appliqué. . . . This is obviously the classic style of the natural school, and its purity, suggestiveness, and beauty must commend it to everyone."

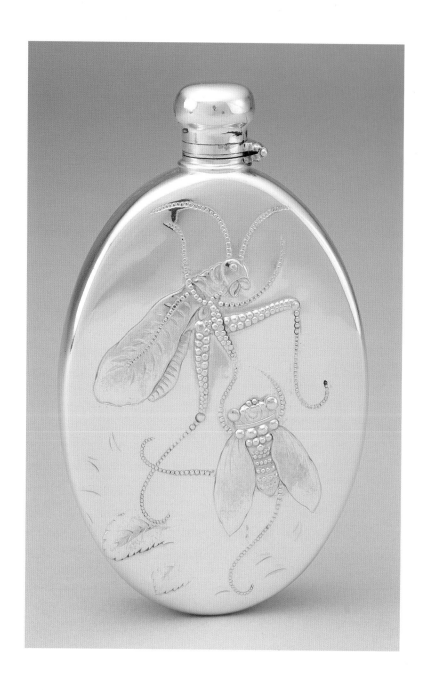

☞ ABOVE: Flask with a grasshopper and a bee. Designed by Charles Osborne circa 1886, the cartoonlike images are almost entirely rendered in pearling. LEFT: hammering and pearling design for this flask.☜

OPPOSITE:

☞ Fish salver designed by Charles Osborne circa 1882. Here Osborne managed to include a spiral of pearling into his highly stylized representation of a fish.☜

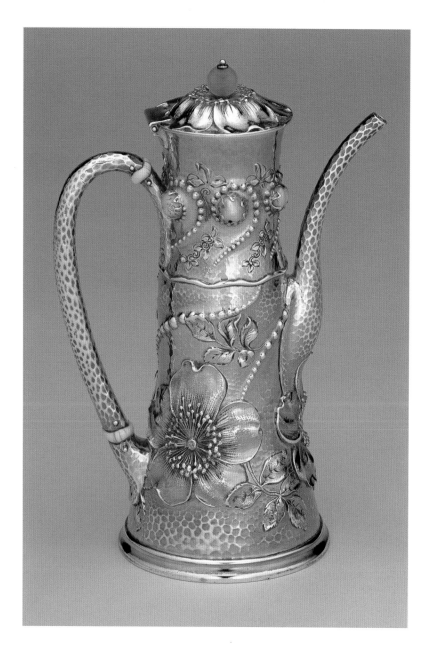

ABOVE:

An 1885 illustration of a similar coffeepot with a spiral of pearling around a poppy.

ABOVE:

This 7-inch-tall after-dinner coffeepot circa 1882 is by Charles Osborne. His designs often employed pearling in spiraling configurations, but this pot is embellished with actual pearls. Osborne was also fond of wild roses, which he used on this piece and more extensively on the salver illustrated on page 159. The coffeepot's range of textures is further extended by hand hammering and a chalcedony finial on the lid.

RIGHT:

Charles Osborne's drawing for a coffeepot nearly identical to the one above. Note his indication for vertical rows of pearling around the top.

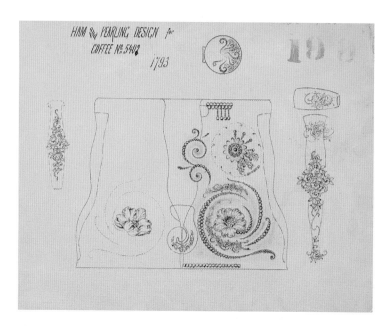

Mokume mantle clock, 9 inches square. A drawing for this clock in the Tiffany Archives is dated November 24, 1880. This is metal-working of astounding virtuosity: the body contains five different *mokume* patterns in forty panels that were welded together and then bent into curving forms. The base is decorated with dogwood blossoms (a favorite motif of Charles Osborne), and the dial is etched with an abstract floral pattern. The clock sold at Christie's on October 1, 1988 for $18,700.

Mokume mustard pot, closely related to the mantel clock above, probably designed by Charles Osborne.

Ewer decorated with seaweed, designed by Charles Osborne and made between 1879 and 1884. The author of "Artistic Silverware" in the Spring 1885 issue of *The Connoisseur* wrote, "The artist has taken the Ammonite [the fossil of an extinct squid-like creature with a spiral shell], and has turned it into a flat spiral whorl of beaded pearls, and he has covered it with a surface treatment suggesting the most delicate sea scum— *confervae*, I believe. Then on each side of the whorls are branches of sea-weed copied perfectly from Nature, for here the object arranged itself, and did not require coaxing and fixing. The throat of the vase is decorated with another kind of sea-weed with shorter filaments and closer seed pods. Below there comes a band of scallop shells which join charmingly with the sea-weed on the body of the vase. Much of the silver is left bare, and the surface is simply *martelé* [hand-hammered], and treated with an acid. Art in the nineteenth century will not surpass this vase in any essential quality of silver working."

The race for the 1885 Goelet Cup for Schooners took place on August 3. A very strong easterly forced two of the four competitors to withdraw, one with her fore-topmast and jib boom blown overboard. The winner was the *Fortuna*, owned by H. S. Hovey of Boston. The trophy, undoubtedly designed by Charles Osborne, is a 28½-inch-tall ewer. In 1885 it was described in an article on yachting trophies in *The Decorator and Furnisher*: "The lip is a representation of a sea-shell with scalloped edges, ending on either side in a spiral similar to that of a nautilus. From this point rises a handle wrought in the resemblance of a fish, whose tail joins the piece below. The neck is ornamented with laurel wreathes festooned over spirally-twisted gadroons, the latter slightly strewn with *repoussé* seaweed. Shells alternating with sea-foliage complete the neck. Then follows a nearly flat surface, wrought out in the semblance of the sea, with dolphins sporting in the water, all in low relief. A procession of mermaids form the drum. Each of them carries her right arm hanging by her side, and the left hand holding a sea-shell at her mouth with cheeks distended, they are sounding a blast upon the shells, and the shells themselves stand out in entire relief, and with the heads of the mermaids form a unique border for the upper edge of the drum. The hair and the bodies of the mermaids, as well as the shallow spaces between them, is strewn with sea-foliage. Their tails twist spirally downward, being drawn inward to form the stem, and again expanding to create a base with their terminations of fins. . . . It cannot be disputed that imagination has asserted itself . . . with a power unerringly positive in its expression, and yet with a delicacy commensurate with the materials." (November 1, 1885) This trophy has come up for auction three times and most recently sold for $151,000 on January 20, 1998, at Sotheby's.

The Orchid Vase, Tiffany's most important showpiece in silver at the 1889 Paris Exposition, was designed by Edward C. Moore—with the probable collaboration of John T. Curran—to complement the twenty-four orchid brooches that were the centerpiece of Tiffany's jewelry display at the Exposition; the vase and the brooches were decorated with matte enamels that Moore had developed. *The Jewelers' Weekly* described the vase: "The etched and enameled vase . . . is 27 inches high, and is a fitting climax to the enameled pieces in the exhibition. Its largest diameter is 16 inches. It is 'Saracenic' in form. The upper part of the body is formed of twelve melon shaped flutes, six large and six small, arranged alternately and receding toward the bottom, where the base is round. The body of the piece is seamless, having been hammered from single sheet of silver to avoid a solder line, which might have affected the process of enameling. The larger flutes are decorated with masses of interlaced orchids enameled in natural colors. The smaller intervening flutes are decorated with Saracenic designs, etched in very bold relief. Underlying the whole of these designs is a diaper [overall pattern] of very shallow etching, forming a splendid background for the bolder designs in relief and enamel. This vase is beyond question the largest and also the handsomest piece of enameled silver ever produced in this country or perhaps in the world. The price affixed to it is $4,000." (May 30, 1889) The vase was purchased by Phoebe Apperson Hearst, wife of California mining magnate and U.S. Senator George Hearst and mother of publisher William Randolph Hearst. In 1891 Mrs. Hearst had Tiffany's refit the vase as an oil lamp with a silver shade and base, and she displayed the lamp in her mansion in Washington, D.C. The lamp later passed to her son, who displayed it in La Cuesta Encantada in San Simeon, California; at his death in 1951 it was appraised at only $500. The Hearst Castle became an historical monument in 1958, and in 1971 its curator wrote Tiffany's an inquiry to which executive vice president LaBar P. Hoagland replied that its replacement value was about $50,000 but failed to identify it as the Orchid Vase from the 1889 Paris Exposition. It was so identified in July 2000, in the course of the research for this book.

The Magnolia Vase, the major showpiece of Tiffany's silver display at the Chicago World's Columbian Exposition of 1893 (and since 1899 owned by the Metropolitan Museum of Art, where it is now on permanent display), is John Curran's masterpiece; and, for its creation alone he would deserve a place of fame in the history of American silver and design.

John T. Curran was of humble origins, born in the Greenpoint section of Brooklyn, New York, on March 31, 1859. His parents, John Curran and Isabelle Griffin Curran, had in 1843 emigrated from Ireland to Brooklyn where John Curran established himself as a stone mason at 106 Newell Street, only two blocks from Charles Grosjean's family dwelling at 154 Norman Avenue, which was on the corner of Newell Street.

While Curran was in his mid-teens, Charles Grosjean must somehow have been instrumental in introducing his neighbor's son to Tiffany & Co. At the Tiffany School, the nineteen-year-old Curran is first noted as the winner of the third prize for the "design for a teapot" in a competition "for prizes of money for excellent specimens of workmanship executed entirely by the apprentices in the several departments of their silverware workshops." (*New York Sun*, September 29, 1878) Curran won ten dollars. The judges included such distinguished names as E. J. Soligny and F. Antoine Heller.

John T. Curran was only eight months older than the Tiffany School's other most distinguished student, Paulding Farnham, and both would follow Edward C. Moore's teachings; however, from his love of spiraling forms and patterns and from the lavish use of Art Nouveau's whiplash curves, undulations, and tendrils in his designs, it is apparent that the young Curran was greatly influenced throughout most of the 1880s by Charles Osborne.

As has been noted, it is clear that Osborne made a contribution to the elaborate, enameled Saracenic silverwares shown by Tiffany's at the Paris Exposition of 1889, and drawings by Curran in the Tiffany Archives confirm that Curran made his own significant contribution to the enameled Saracenic wares; but for Tiffany's the two stars of that exposi-

John T. Curran's watercolor of an orchid for the Orchid Vase. Signed at lower left with his cipher—the letters "JTC" superimposed upon each other—and dated December 7, 1888.

John T. Curran's watercolors of flowers for the Magnolia Vase. OPPOSITE, BOTTOM: labeled "Umbrella Magnolia May-16-91." ABOVE: "Magnolia Study May-1-91." BELOW: "Goldenrod" dated September 11, 1891; this watercolor has Curran's cipher at bottom right.

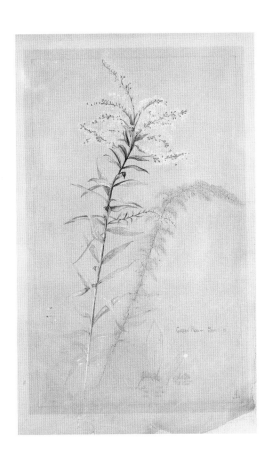

tion were Edward C. Moore, whose silverware won the grand prize, and Paulding Farnham, whose jewelry for Tiffany's won a gold medal.

Osborne, of course, had left Tiffany & Co. to return to Whiting over one year before the opening of the Exposition, and therefore would have received no credit from Tiffany & Co. for his role. Curran was equally ignored despite the importance of his contributions, which included the enameling patterns for the the Orchid Vase, the exhibit's centerpiece, as well as for a matching tea set, and numerous other pieces of the Saracenic silver exhibited. The Orchid Vase, with its six panels of polychromed enameled orchids echoed the collection of twenty-four enameled and jeweled orchid brooches and hair ornaments that Paulding Farnam was preparing for his jewelry display. The six gouache enameling patterns for the Orchid Vase still in the Tiffany Archives have nervous, uncertain brushwork that corresponds to Curran's floral renderings in the archives. They are certainly by Curran and presage his work on the Magnolia Vase that followed soon after.

One year after the exposition, Curran would receive his first significant recognition for his flatsilver pattern "Broom Corn" (U.S. Patent No 20173, September 30, 1890). "Broom Corn" has intrigued the world of design for its apparent proto–Art Nouveau inspiration from an all-but-unknown design book entitled *Essay on Broom-Corn* published in Dayton, Ohio, in 1887 by Edward Colonna, a young architect-designer who had collaborated with Louis Comfort Tiffany earlier in the 1880s. (He later collaborated with Tiffany's friend Siegfried Bing at La Maison d'Art Nouveau, where about 1897 Colonna designed silver-gilt art mountings for Tiffany's Favrile glass pieces.)

How Curran came by Colonna's essay on the decorative applications of the undulating, curling, and interweaving pannicles of a type of sorghum (known as "broom corn" since besoms were often made from it) is unclear. Perhaps the young Colonna (b. 1862, Cologne, Germany) sent a copy of his essay to his former employer Louis Comfort Tiffany, who passed it on to Edward C. Moore for use in the Tiffany School. In any case, it influenced John T. Curran and reinforced the penchant he inherited from John Osborne for proto–Art Nouveau design, as witnessed by his "Broom Corn" flatsilver, conceived of and designed about 1889, after work for the Paris Exposition was completed, and patented in 1890.

Charles Lewis Tiffany and Edward C. Moore had the highest regard for Curran's abilities; at Edward C. Moore's death in 1891, Curran succeeded him as head of silver design at Tiffany's.

In this new position, Curran would devote all of his considerable talents and energies to the design and production of silverware to be exhibited at the World's Columbian Exposition of 1893. He would be aided in this by Tiffany's new chief jewelry designer Paulding Farnham, as well as by the firm's older silversmiths, James Whitehouse and Eugene Soligny.

Curran's masterpiece for the Chicago World's Fair of 1893 was, as noted, his magnificent enameled and jeweled Magnolia Vase, but there were many other magnificent John T. Curran designs shown in Tiffany's display of 1893; they would again merit Tiffany & Co. the grand prize for silverware. These included two extraordinary Art Nouveau jeweled vases, both bought by the Kunstgewerbemuseum in Berlin, where they remain to this day. The first, the Nautical Vase, a baroque pearl-studded baluster-form vase with spiraling seaweed motifs and seashell feet, remains closest to the work of Charles Osborne but with a tension—and at once an exuberance—to the composition, as well as with an asymmetry verging on randomness unknown in Osborne's work. The second, the Tarpon Vase, is to some extent, like the Magnolia Vase, based in its form on antique Native American pottery. It is set with six large curved pear-shape aquamarines surrounded by parcel gilt seaweed motifs all caught up in a powerful, writhing whorl of streamlined and stylized fish.

There was a series of small, whimsical, Symbolist-inspired vases covered with owls' heads, bats with wings outstretched against a blue enamel sky, spiraling snails or "Japanesque turtles"; an overall enameled, rather Japanesque Falcon Vase using, like the Magnolia Vase, the subtle but rich palette of pale matte enamels that Edward C. Moore had developed for his Saracenic enameled silver; a remarkable Florida Tankard with deep repoussé-chased oranges surrounded by rather menacing tropical flora outdoing Osborne at his own game (probably with considerable help in chasing from Soligny); a Daisy Vase, most of its surface covered with a nervous fabric of yellow-and-white daisy flowerheads on silver stems with spiraling silver roots about its base and a crenellation of white daisies at its lip, in composition relating to both the Magnolia Vase and to the series of owls and bats and various other

John T. Curran designed the 31-inch-tall Magnolia Vase for the 1893 Chicago Exposition. Tiffany's priced it at $10,000 and its catalogue stated, "The form was suggested by a piece of pottery found among the relics of the ancient cliff-dwellers of the New Mexican Pueblos. The decorations are chased in relief-work, and some treated in enameling. Around the base or foot of the vase are four large pieces of opal matrix representing the earth, out of which springs a lattice-work of cactus leaves chased in high relief; these are divided into sections by perfectly wrought golden-rod, pure gold being used to reproduce the natural color. The roots of the flower terminate in scrolls encircling the opals. Above the growth of cactus leaves and golden-rod, matted as a solid decoration around the widest part of the vase, is a frieze of magnolias enameled in natural size and colors, showing all the delicate tints, with the soft, subdued effect as in life. The pine cones and needles around the top and neck of the vase typify the north and east, the magnolias represent the mid-south and west, the cacti the sub-tropical region, and the golden-rod the national flower, which grows in all four sections of the country. Nearly a thousand dollars' worth of gold was used in the representation of the golden-rod. The vase measures 17 inches in diameter as its widest part, and weighs 777 ounces (about 65 pounds)." Charles A. Dana, editor of the *New York Sun*, wrote that it "impresses the beholder as one of the most remarkable specimens of the silversmith and author art that has ever been produced anywhere," but the French silversmith and author André Bouilhet called it "a too confusing composition. Its execution is extraordinarily remarkable; but what a lot of difficulties have been vanquished for so small a result." The vase was purchased by Cornelia Ann Atwill, who left it to the Metropolitan Museum of Art in 1901.

eccentric creatures; and there was a "Broom Corn" bowl and matching plate all writhing and whorling with the tendrils of Colonna's broom-corn.

With his prize-winning display at the World's Columbian Exposition of 1893, Curran was at his peak, from which he apparently quickly was toppled by 1890s Tiffany politics.

Following the exposition, he continued as head of the design department at the Prince Street silverworks, but in 1897 moved to the new Tiffany silver factory at Forest Hill, Newark, New Jersey, where he was again head of the new factory's design department, but apparently subordinate to Paulding Farnham in New York. Little is known of him after this. Brooklyn city directories indicate that he returned to Brooklyn two years later, but it is not clear that he remained in the employ of Tiffany's. In 1903 his place of business is listed as 860 Broadway, on the northeast corner of Broadway and Union Square, two blocks north of Tiffany's Union Square store.

After Edward C. Moore's death in 1891 had he been put in a position of competition for design leadership with Paulding Farnham, who had the full support of Charles Lewis Tiffany as well as that of his uncle, Tiffany's president, Charles T. Cook? It is possible that following Charles Lewis Tiffany's death in 1902 the tide turned against him, as it did for his contemporary, Paulding Farnham. Was his penchant for Art Nouveau design too close to or somehow in competition with the Art Nouveau designs of Tiffany's new and world-famous design director, Louis Comfort Tiffany?

There is no sign of Curran's remarkably inventive, if somewhat tense and troubled, hand in Tiffany's silverwares for either the Paris World's Fair of 1900 or the Pan-American Exposition held in Buffalo, New York, in 1901; and history is silent on any later work of this designer who was so brilliant in his youth and who, at the age of thirty-four, brought honor and distinction to Tiffany & Co. at the Chicago World's Fair of 1893.

John T. Curran, then living in the Stapleton section of Staten Island at 110 Boyd Street and simply calling himself an "artist," died at St. Vincent's Hospital on Staten Island on March 26, 1933, five days before his seventy-fourth birthday. The event went unnoticed by the press, although his works were in the collections of at least two of the world's great museums, and he was the author of what is arguably the single greatest piece of Art Nouveau silver produced in the United States, the Magnolia Vase.

John T. Curran's Owl Vase designed for the 1893 Chicago Exposition. Along with the now-vanished Snail and Terrapin Vases, the Owl Vase was one of three similar 10½-inch-tall vases at the exposition. Their form was listed as "Peruvian" and they were covered with multiple images: the Owl Vase with owls' faces, the Snail Vase with snails' shells, and the Terrapin Vase with the backs of terrapins. Curran embellished the Owl Vase with miniature owls perched on a branch around the lip and talons around the base. (The talons are similar to those at the top of the Falcon Vase on page 188). The French silversmith André Bouilhet commented, "From the neck to the foot, heads of the night bird are alternated and diminish in size as the vase shrinks and is elongated. Other objects of analogous form are decorated with snail, turtles, serpents [an incense burner with a rattlesnake strangling a duck], and produce an unforeseen sensation. I admire more Tiffany in these small pieces, full of wit and imagination, than when he executes works of large dimension [i.e., the Magnolia Vase]." (The Jewelers' Review, October 16, 1893) OPPOSITE, CENTER: Curran's Bat Vase's design is essentially Japanesque, yet it incorporates Limoges enamel insets. Tiffany's catalogue described it, "BAT VASE, form Greek, conventional bats, chased and etched, background of sky, stars and clouds in enamel." OPPOSITE, TOP: Enameling pattern for the Bat Vase.

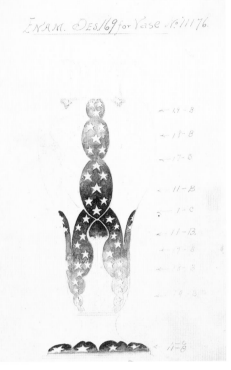

ENAM. DES/69 for Vase No 11176.

PARIS.
BUFFALO.

DIAMONDS
PARIS EXHIBITION
1900.
PAN AMERICAN
EXHIBITION
1901

⌒ The 13-inch-tall Falcon Vase designed by John T. Curran for the 1893 World's Columbian Exposition in Chicago. Tiffany's catalogue described it: "Enameled in colors, after Limoges; body, metal silver; base of vase in applied work of green gold. The body of the vase represents a background of silvery mountain-tops and fleecy clouds, through which a blue sky is seen; while falcons in combat, with out-stretched wings, extend over the front. The whole color effect is produced in enamel-work. The cover of the vase represents a falcon hood, the lower part showing the claws of the bird, and the dome of the cover is in the form of the top-knot on the head of the bird." The New York *Sun* commented, "Ten years ago the pansies and violets in enamel that were here [in the United States] were all imported from France. Six or eight years ago we began attempts to make our own pansies, daisies, and other flowers. . . At the time of the Paris Exposition of 1889 Tiffany & Co. exhibited some orchids in enamel that marked a decided advance. The experimental step that they have now taken is in the form of a vase in Limoges enamel upon silver. It is perhaps only a study, but it is fine." (April 14, 1893, repr. in *The Jewelers' Review*, October 16, 1893) The Falcon Vase was purchased by George Westinghouse, whose Westinghouse Electric Company lit the Chicago Exposition; he and his wife, Marguerite, gave the vase to another couple for Christmas in 1897. It was sold at Sotheby's on June 20, 1996 for $57,500. ⌒

Silver and parcel-gilt vase studded with "old Irish aquamarines" designed by John T. Curran for the 1893 Chicago Exposition. The lip of the vase is a row of inverted tarpon tails, the neck is etched with freshwater weeds, and the base is encircled with tarpon heads. This and the similar Art Nouveau vase below were purchased at the Exposition by the Kunstgewerbemuseum in Berlin, which still has them in its collection.

John T. Curran also designed this 7-inch-tall pearl-studded vase for the 1893 World's Columbian Exposition in Chicago. Tiffany's catalogue described it tersely: "Pearl Vase, form Greek, body silver, set with American pearls and chased seaweeds." The swirling seaweed shows Curran's affinities with the Art Nouveau movement.

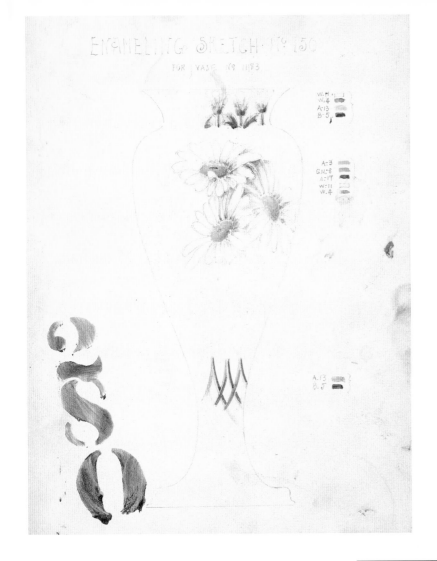

☞ Pitcher designed by Charles Osborne circa 1885, with starfish decoration by John T. Curran, circa 1892. ☜

OPPOSITE:

☞ Designed by John T. Curran for the World's Columbian Exposition in Chicago, the 14½-inch-tall Daisy Vase is covered with white-and-yellow daisies in matte enamels developed by Edward C. Moore; similar enamels had been used to stunning effect on Moore and Curran's Orchid Vase (see page 180) and Paulding Farnham's orchid brooches at the 1889 Paris Exposition. Curran's affinities with the nascent Art Nouveau movement can be seen in the spiraling stems on the foot of the vase. Both the Daisy Vase and the Magnolia Vase (see page 185) were purchased at the Chicago Exposition by Cornelia Ann Atwill (1812–1901). Eighty years old when the Chicago Exposition opened, Mrs. Atwill had up-to-date tastes; she also collected "Favrile" glass objects by Louis Comfort Tiffany. The Daisy Vase sold at Christie's on January 16, 1998 for $85,000. ABOVE: Curran's enameling sketch for the Daisy Vase. ☜

Saracenic loving cup decorated with blue, yellow, and pink enamel, 9⅝ inches tall, made in 1893 for the World's Columbian Exposition in Chicago. It was designed in Edward C. Moore's style by his successor, John T. Curran, whose enameling pattern is at right.)

Made for the 1893 Chicago Exposition, this after-dinner coffeepot was described in Tiffany's catalogue as "style 'Saracenic,' enameled decorations, jade knob on cover." The body's elongated floral decoration and subdued coloration has affinities with Art Nouveau, suggesting that John T. Curran probably designed it. André Bouilhet wrote of the Tiffany display in Chicago, "There is especially a series of small coffeepots of semi-oriental forms and decorations, which is a most interesting attempt; proportions are well studied, forms happily found, and the decorations most successful. They are ornamented with dull enamels with effaced colors, its deaf harmony seeming to suit the subdued tone of oxidized silver. To take coffee in such beautiful jewels must be a very tempting dream too; but at what a price! I strongly urged my friend [jewelry historian Henri] Vever to bring back to Paris one of the most charming specimens; and I intended to seek him, from time to time in the Rue de la Paix, and see whether the aroma of the coffee does not exhaust itself in so handsome a coffee-pot." (*The Jewelers' Review*, October 16, 1893)

Pitcher designed by John T. Curran in 1893, of the same family as his tankard on the opposite page. Another pitcher almost identical to this 9-inch-tall example was shown at the 1893 Chicago Exposition: Tiffany's catalogue listed it, "TROPICAL PITCHER, mounted and chased with cactus, banana, and other tropical plants." This pitcher sold at Christie's East on October 20, 1993 for $17,000.

Designed by John T. Curran for the 1893 Chicago Exposition, this tankard with a hinged cover is decorated with repoussé-chased tropical flora, including oranges, bananas, and magnolias, along with palm fronds and prickly pear cacti repeated from the lower portion of the Magnolia Vase.

Silver-gilt punch bowl circa 1877. The Japanesque bowl, decorated with dragonflies and water lilies, was designed by Edward C. Moore; the polar bears on the base were a much-used model by Eugene J. Soligny.

Ice bowl designed by James H. Whitehouse circa 1867, with three polar bears modeled by Eugene J. Soligny. This was perhaps the first appearance of these polar bears; they reappeared frequently on punch bowls and ice bowls over the next twenty-five years. The John Hancock Bank of Springfield, Massachusetts, presented the bowl to James M. Thompson, who served as the bank's first president from 1850 to 1863. It sold at Sotheby's on December 15, 1998, for $21,850.

Made for the 1893 Chicago Exposition, the base of the "Arctic Ice Bowl" by John T. Curran has two sculpted polar bears among pine boughs and chunks of rock crystal representing ice. These polar bears, first used on the punch bowl above about 1867, were probably modeled by Eugene J. Soligny: he directed silver production for the Chicago Exposition and found this ice bowl an appropriate place for his old, but still popular, figures. The bowl's pine needles and pine cones also appear on the neck of Curran's the Magnolia Vase.

PAULDING FARNHAM

George Paulding Farnham was born at his grandparents' house at 171 Sullivan Street in New York's Greenwich Village on November 6, 1859, to George and Julia Paulding Farnham, both of whose families had been in Connecticut or New York since the seventeenth century.

Farnham's connection to Tiffany & Co. was natural. His maternal aunt, Eleanor Paulding Cook, was the first wife of the founder Charles Lewis Tiffany's right-hand man, Charles Thomas Cook, Tiffany's vice president from 1868 to 1902 and president from 1902 to 1907.

Born the same year as John T. Curran, Farnham would also have become an apprentice and student in Edward C. Moore's Tiffany School about 1875. While Curran was a disciple of Charles Osborne, Farnham was a disciple of Moore. He graduated from his apprenticeship to the coveted post of general assistant to Moore on November 1, 1885, five days before his twenty-sixth birthday. Five days later, the newsweekly *New York Town Topics* noted "a design of Paul Farnham" in Tiffany's new jewelry offerings. It was a "natural sized" enameled gold Japanese chrysanthemum brooch with a brilliant-cut yellow diamond at its center. This almost unheard-of mention of a Tiffany designer's name in the press speaks to the admiration Tiffany's and Moore must have had for the young designer's talents.

A little over a year later, by early 1887, Tiffany's would be focusing its attentions on preparations for the great Universal Exposition to be held in Paris in 1889 commemorating the one-hundredth anniversary of the French Revolution. Paulding Farnham was chosen to use his best efforts on the Tiffany jewelry collections to be displayed in 1889. This he did with great distinction. His collections of some two hundred jewels and jeweled objects, a large number of them based on Native American Indian design, won Tiffany's a gold medal for jewelry.

The silverware collections for 1889 would focus on Edward C. Moore's enameled "Saracenic" wares, and in designing these he had the brilliantly capable and imaginative assistance of John T. Curran. James Whitehouse, Eugene Soligny, Charles Grosjean, and Charles Osborne were, of course, all designing in Tiffany's silver department at the same time and would have contributed to the project. However, as

Trophy for the winner of the Belmont Stakes in 1896. It was commissioned by August ("Augie") Belmont II in honor of his father, who had established the Belmont Stakes in 1867 and died in 1891. Designed by Paulding Farnham, the trophy's oak leaf decoration and acorn form—symbolizing the origins of thoroughbred bloodlines ("great oaks from little acorns grow")—appears to have been based on Paul Storr's centerpiece made in London in 1836 for Lord Hatherton. The horse forming the handle of the lid represents the senior August Belmont's Fenian, who won the Belmont Stakes in 1869. The horses represented on the base of the cup—Eclipse, Herod, and Matchem—were bred in England in the eighteenth century, and every thoroughbred in the world today is descended from one of these three. Farnham used photographs of Augie Belmont's horses— Hastings, Henry of Navarre, and Merry Prince—to model these horses. When Hastings won the Belmont Stakes on June 2, 1896, Augie Belmont ordered two cases of wine opened to christen the Tiffany cup that he had commissioned. In 1926 his heirs donated it to the Jockey Club as the perpetual trophy for the Belmont Stakes.

LEFT:

Saracenic silver-gilt coffee set designed by Paulding Farnham circa 1900. The coffeepot, sugar bowl, and creamer have interlaced ovals of half-pearls around sage green champlevé enamel arabesque foliage. The oval tray, listed in Tiffany's records for 1905 as "to go with coffee set," has the initial "M" in the center: it is believed to stand for the a member of the family of Andrew Mellon, the Pittsburgh financier, art collector, and philanthropist.

OPPOSITE:

Designed by Paulding Farnham and completed in 1895, the Adams Vase was the centerpiece of Tiffany & Co.'s display at the 1900 Exposition Universelle in Paris, where one critic called it "a masterpiece of the goldsmith's art and a triumph for Mr. Farnham, the designer and modeller..." (*The Art Interchange*) In 1893 the board of directors of the American Cotton Oil Company commissioned Tiffany's to make the vase in honor of their chairman, Edward Dean Adams, who saved the firm from bankruptcy and declined any compensation. The board stipulated that it be "produced from materials exclusively American": thus the yellow-green gold was mined in Forest City, California, the approximately two hundred semiprecious gems—quartzes, spessartites, amethysts, tourmalines, and freshwater pearls—all came from the United States, and the base is California gold quartz. The decorative motifs are based on Farnham's drawings of cotton blossoms and branches; the partly nude female figure on this side of the vase represents Modesty, and the male figure on the opposite side represents Genius. Farnham himself wrote, "The two youthful figures on the foot represent the young Atlas turning the financial world at his pleasure, his hand resting on the ornamental beaver to convey the idea that he is sensitive to the presence and importance of industry. The opposite figure represents the new country and Husbandry, holding a cotton-branch in his hand." Adams presented the vase to New York's Metropolitan Museum of Art in 1904.

the Paris Exposition neared, Charles Osborne left Tiffany & Co., and Charles Grosjean died less than two months later. This left Edward C. Moore to depend more heavily on John T. Curran and Paulding Farnham than he would have imagined when preparations began at the end of 1886.

There are no records as to the precise roles Curran and Farnham played in designing the silver for the 1889 fair; however, Farnham's exhibitor's pass (#882 from the French Ministry of Commerce and Industry) lists him in three categories: "Class 24—Goldsmith's and silversmith's work... silver ware for house hold use, the table, the toilet, and for ornament, decorated with chasing, etching, niello, enameling, jeweling, and inlays of metal; Class 29—Leather work; and Class 37—Jewelry and precious stones."

The only silver safely attributable to Farnham that drew attention at the 1889 fair would be the Buffalo Loving Cups; they began the series of magnificent silver bowls and vases in

Designed by Paulding Farnham, the Viking Punch Bowl commemorating pre-Columbian explorations of North America was one of the most important pieces shown at the 1893 Chicago Exposition. Tiffany's catalogue listed its material as "decarbonized iron," meaning iron that has been heated to a very high temperature to eliminate virtually all carbon content in order to make it malleable. The iron of this bowl was hammered and "damascened" (inlaid with complex patterns in gold and silver). Its eight handles pass through the lip to terminate in shapes like the prows of Viking ships. The bowl is 20¼ inches in diameter, and the interior is plain silver. It was evidently purchased at the Chicago Exposition by John Crossley of Sussex, England and is now at the Metropolitan Museum of Art in New York.

Designed by Paulding Farnham, this silver and ebony oval punch bowl with a swinging handle was completed on November 19, 1902. The four roundels in the central band around the body are set with black opals. This impressive 18-inch-long bowl may have been commissioned by a client who admired Farnham's gem-studded "Viking" wares at the 1901 Buffalo Exposition. It sold for $46,000 at Christie's on January 26, 1995.

Native American Indian style that Farnham would design for the World's Columbian Exposition of 1893 and for the Paris Exposition of 1900.

At Edward C. Moore's death in 1891, Paulding Farnham became head of jewelry at Tiffany's (senior to John T. Curran, head of silverware), and later that year, he designed an elaborate enameled gold loving cup commemorating the golden wedding anniversary of Mr. and Mrs. Charles Lewis Tiffany (November 30, 1891), a commission that should have more logically gone to the head silver designer, Curran.

Farnham would also design a significant collection of exhibition pieces for the World's Columbian Exposition. There Tiffany's would show his series of extraordinary niello-and-copper inlayed, or enameled and gem-encrusted, American Indian–style "Pueblo" bowls; and there his first pieces in his "Viking" style would be exhibited, including the Viking Bowl now in the collections of the Metropolitan Museum of Art.

Although Curran won the gold medal for silver for Tiffany & Co. at the 1893 fair, it was Paulding Farnham who received the commissions for the most important presentation pieces Tiffany's would make in the remainder of the 1890s: the Adams Vase (completed 1895), the most splendid Renaissance Revival–style object made in America, and the Belmont Cup (completed 1896), America's most famous horse-racing trophy. On permanent display at the Metropolitan Museum since

1904, the jeweled and enameled gold Adams Vase was first presented to the public as the central showpiece of Tiffany's display at the Paris Exposition of 1900.

At the time of the 1900 fair, Farnham was in charge, not just of jewelry, but of all Tiffany design, and his designs would win Tiffany's the grand prize for jewelry as well as the grand prize for silverware. The silverware included three splendid American Indian–style turquoise-encrusted vases by Farnham: the Navajo Vase, the Zuni Bowl, and the Hupa Bowl. In the prizewinning Tiffany display, there was also a set of highly imaginative silver objects, including a dressing-table mirror, two wine coolers, and two candlesticks in a new "Burmese" style of silver; a dressing table set in a "Russian" style; a monumental beer flagon of carved ivory mounted with silver elephants and crocodiles, and with sculpted silver rattlesnakes forming its handle; a "Pompeian" oxidized and enameled silver vase; "Egyptian" and "Byzantine" enameled coffeepots with jade finials; a "Viking" jewel box; loving cups with Bighorn sheep horns or buffalo horns as handles; vases in "New Zealand," "Viking," and "Celtic" styles; a tall, elegant silver vase with "Greek Gentian, treated in blue gold." There was no style of silver design that Farnham was not at home with; and many of the styles, although named for other cultures, seemed to be purely of his own invention. Farnham also collaborated with Louis Comfort Tiffany on mountings for a series of Tiffany's "Favrile" glass vases. Farnham designed jeweled Renaissance Revival mounts that were in a design style highly unlikely to please Louis Comfort Tiffany.

A number of the silver showpieces from the 1900 fair would be shown again by Farnham and Tiffany's at the Pan-American Exposition held in Buffalo in 1901, where Tiffany's silverwares would again win the gold medal. More of Farnham's jeweled "Viking" style pieces would be produced for the Buffalo World's Fair, and some would continue on to the Turin International Exposition of Modern Decorative Arts of 1902, where Tiffany displayed but did not compete.

Then in 1902, Farnham's luck, like Curran's before him, changed. His patron Charles Lewis Tiffany died, and control of Tiffany's was taken by his celebrated designer son, Louis Comfort Tiffany, who named himself design director, displacing Farnham. Louis Comfort Tiffany clearly had no patience with the younger Farnham's celebrity as a designer and no intention of sharing the spotlight with him.

Although Farnham would continue to design jewelry, most-

✐ Full-length mirror made for the 1900 Paris Exposition. Tiffany's catalogue listed it: "Mounted in silver, mahogany wood frame, covered with pierced silver ornament with candelabra at the top of each side and a small service-tray on each upright support." ✐

ly in a detailed early Edwardian style, and continued to design elaborately enameled and jeweled silverware such as the magnificent silver gilt and vivid pink enamel coffee set studded with amethysts of 1902 (now in the High Museum, Atlanta, Georgia), he designed only one necklace for the Louisiana Purchase Exhibition of 1904, in the Renaissance Revival style, and his silver design focused on an immense and elaborate Renaissance Revival hollowware service, quite out of step with the Art Nouveau and arts and crafts tastes of his employer.

Farnham stayed on at Tiffany's, though, apparently under the protection of his uncle, Tiffany's president Charles T. Cook. Cook, however, died at seventy-one on January 26, 1907. Nothing is known of Paulding Farnham's last year at Tiffany & Co. He resigned his post on June 2, 1908, at only forty-eight years of age.

For the remainder of his life, Paulding Farnham devoted his efforts to sculpture and painting, curiously never returning to either jewelry or silver design. He died at sixty-eight on August 10, 1927, at Agnew State Hospital in Santa Clara County, California.

Farhnam's work at the end of the nineteenth century had brought Tiffany & Co. and the United States international respect as the undisputed leader in jewelry design and succeeded in sustaining the position of world leader in silver design that Edward C. Moore has established for Tiffany & Co. in the 1878 and 1889 Paris Expositions.

≈ "Viking" vase decorated with enamels and studded with opals. Designed by Paulding Farnham, possibly for the 1901 Pan-American Exposition in Buffalo. It was shown again in 1902 at the Turin Exposition. *≈*

≈ "Viking" coffee service designed by Paulding Farnham for the 1901 Pan-American Exposition in Buffalo; it was shown again in 1902 at the International Exposition of Modern Decorative Arts in Turin. It has interlacing Celtic-derived designs with pale-green and lavender enamels and is studded with zircons and hessonite garnets. *≈*

Buffalo loving cup, probably designed circa 1889 by
Edward C. Moore and Paulding Farnham, with handles in
the form of bison horns resting upon bison heads and hooves
modeled by Eugene J. Soligny for the Bennett Candelabra in
1875 (see page 113). The body and the handles are inlaid with
bold, abstract Native American designs in copper and niello.
The gilt interior has an engraved sunburst at the center.
These cups were stylistic forerunners of Farnham's great
Native American designs of 1893–1900.

ABOVE:

Paulding Farnham designed several "Pueblo" vases for the 1893 Chicago Exposition, basing their shapes and patterns on pottery made by the Pueblo tribes of New Mexico and Arizona; *The Jewelers' Review* called them "very beautiful in execution and finish." The shoulder of this example has four engraved clusters of greasewood, sagebrush, sacred thorn, and mesquite.

TOP LEFT:

Detail of the bottom of the vase.

BOTTOM LEFT:

Detail of "sacred thorn" cluster on the shoulder of the vase.

A smaller "Pueblo" vase by Farnham, which differs from all the other examples in that it is studded with rubies; its patterns are yellow, pink, and green enamel rather than copper and niello; and its base is inscribed "Souvenir of America from Nellie."

Farnham based this vase for the 1900 Paris Exposition on Navajo pottery. The shoulder and the lower body are studded with American turquoises and "Amazon stones"; the "corn cob" handles contain 322 American freshwater pearls.

BELOW:

Designed by Paulding Farnham for the 1900 Paris Exposition, this bowl inlaid with niello and studded with turquoises was based on baskets made by the Zuni tribe in New Mexico. One critic thought Farnham's Native American–inspired pieces surpassed his more conventional designs: "In silver articles nothing more original either in shape or in treatment could be found than the bowls, hammered out by hand from single pieces of silver, following the shapes of Zuni and Hupa Indian baskets. . . . To the artist's eye they seem better worth the thought and care bestowed upon them than the more elaborate Adams Vase." (*The Art Interchange*, May 1900.)

≈ Bowl designed by Paulding Farnham for the
1900 Paris Exposition. Tiffany's catalogue listed
it as, "Silver and copper. Hammered up by hand,
of one piece. Shape taken from a Hupa Indian
basket. Style of silver inlaying represents a flight
of wild birds. The handles are conventional
rattle-snakes, set with American turquoise." ≈

⌇ This silver and copper wine cooler, probably designed by Paulding Farnham and made in 1900, is a superb example of the wave of neoclassicism that swept America following the lead of the 1893 Chicago Exposition. Its shape and scrolled handles are taken from ancient Greek kraters, vessels used for mixing wine with water. Like other works of Greek pottery, kraters were colored red, black, and white: this wine cooler's chaste coloration and exquisitely wrought decoration are characteristic of turn-of-the-century neoclassicism. ⌇

Enameled silver "Pompeian" vase, 16 ⅞ inches tall, designed by Paulding Farnham for the 1900 Paris Exposition. This vase's coloration and exuberant handles set it apart from the severe neoclassicism of the wine cooler on the opposite page made at about the same time. The vase was originally oxidized, giving it the handsome patina of ancient silver. Unfortunately an early owner decided to have it brightly polished. Tiffany's made another version of this vase as the trophy for a balloon race sponsored by the Aero Club of the United Kingdom held in Paris in September 1906.

Designed by Paulding Farnham, this huge (27½-inch-tall) exhibition tankard was made for the 1900 Paris Exposition. *The New York Times* commented, "Another specially attractive exhibit is an ivory-carved, silver-mounted tankard. The carving in ivory is very elaborate. The base is a wonder of silver hand craftsmanship, being wrought into a phalanx of exquisitely carved elephants which rest upon a dais consisting of a design of marvelously depicted crocodiles. A massive elephant, beaten in silver, surmounts the tankard." (September 18, 1900) The handle is formed of intertwined snakes, and the body has a scene of fighting gorillas. The extraordinary ivory carving was the work of Joseph Fischer, who emigrated from Germany in 1881 and worked at Tiffany's from 1892 until 1906. He then worked independently on medallions and on silver and ivory presentation pieces, some even more elaborate than this tankard. The Pabst Brewing Co. purchased the tankard (perhaps at the Paris Exposition). Pabst sold it to the Tiffany Archives at a Sotheby's on-line auction that closed on April 26, 2001.

Tiffany's completed this 13¾-inch-long cigar box on August 6, 1900. An elephant forms the handle of the lid of the box, whose sides are decorated with bas-relief elephants in various poses against a background of embossed trees and mountaintops. Elephants were popular motifs in the late nineteenth century, particularly for pieces intended for men: other elephant-decorated examples of Tiffany silver include an 1874 elephant water pitcher and a footed bowl (see page 123), an elephant loving cup shown at the 1889 Paris Exposition, and an elephant tankard shown at the 1900 Paris Exposition (above). This cigar box sold at Sotheby's for $71,500 on October 22, 1988.

The "Aztec Calendar-Plate" was made for the 1893 Chicago Exposition, where it was apparently purchased by William Randolph Hearst, then the brilliant thirty-year-old publisher of the *San Francisco Examiner*. *The Collector* reported, "It is . . . circular in shape, with a diameter of 18 inches, and on the metal is etched a copy of the figures of the famous Aztec stone of the City of Mexico, the scene of so many bloody human sacrifices. . . . The theories regarding the significance of the signs and symbols found upon the Aztec stone calendar indicates the central face as representing the sun, the circles of symbols around the center represent the early Mexican method of recording time, and the two serpents forming the outside border are supposed to be symbolic of heaven or eternity." (August 1, 1893, repr. *The Jewelers' Review*, October 16, 1893) Around the perimeter of the tray are an openwork apron and ten step supports surmounted by agates carved in the form of scallop shells. The tray sold for $36,300 at Sotheby's in January 1988.

TOP AND ABOVE:

✍ This coffee set was part of a monumental Renaissance Revival service that Paulding
Farnham designed for the 1904 Louisiana Purchase Exposition in St. Louis. The handles
of the standing pieces were formed of winged female figures based on similar figures
by the painter and designer Hans Holbein the Younger (1497?–1543), an artist Farnham
seems to have much admired as he also produced at least one jewel after a Holbein
design. This service was a success, and the following year Tiffany's made additional
pieces such as the vegetable dish at top. ✜

Hans Holbein the Younger's drawing for an elaborate cup made for Jane Seymour in 1536, the year she became Henry VIII's third wife. The drawing appears to have been an inspiration for Paulding Farnham's Renaissance Revival silver shown at the 1904 St. Louis Exposition.

LOVING CUP PRESENTED TO
MR. JAMES T. WOODWARD
BY HIS ASSOCIATES OF THE HANOVER NATIONAL BANK
TIFFANY & CO. NEW YORK MAKERS
JUNE 1901.

Archival photograph of the elaborately decorated loving cup presented by the directors and officers of the Hanover National Bank to its president, James T. Woodward, in June 1901. Stylistic affinities with the Adams Vase of 1893–95 suggest that it was designed by Paulding Farnham. James T. Woodward, who came from an old Maryland family, was elected the bank's president in 1877 and turned it into a highly profitable and widely respected institution. He never married, and upon his death in 1910 was succeeded as president by his nephew William Woodward, who also inherited his Belair Farm in Bowie, Maryland. William Woodward established a stud at Belair that produced two Triple Crown winners, Gallant Fox and Omaha. The Hanover National Bank was one of the forerunners of the present-day Chase Manhattan Corporation.

The engineer John B. McDonald's $35 million bid won New York's contract to construct the city's first subway line in 1899. On February 21, 1900, McDonald and financier August Belmont formed the Rapid Transit Construction Company to execute the contract, and on May 24 Mayor Robert A. Van Wyck used a silver Tiffany commemorative shovel at the groundbreaking ceremony near City Hall. In 1902, under a lease from the city, Belmont formed the Interborough Rapid Transit Company to operate the subway. The subway's inaugural run took place on October 27, 1904. At a banquet that evening, Interborough Rapid Transit's board of directors presented Belmont with this 38-inch-long tray with handles representing shovels and pickaxes. Belmont's portrait medallion is at the top, and a line of subway track forms the border around the map showing the IRT's lines in Manhattan and the Bronx.

Commissioned by August Belmont, Jr., this tray was designed by Paulding Farnham for the winner of the 1901 running of the Belmont Stakes; Farnham designed all the Belmont Stakes trophies awarded between 1896 and 1907. The handles are formed as bridles and the sides are decorated with palm fronds, the symbols of victory. It was won by James R. Keene's Commando at Morris Park on May 23, 1901. *The New York Times* reported: "Under ideal conditions, with a magnificent crowd in attendance and over a track that was lightening fast, the two colts esteemed by shrewd judges to be the best in America, Commando and The Parader [owned by Richard T. Wilson, Jr., Mrs. William Astor's son-in-law], met for the thirty-fifth running of the Belmont Stakes at Morris Park yesterday. The result of the race in every way was as splendid as the promise the contest made, the winner, Commando, setting a new record for the event and for the course, and romping home in a style that compelled even the partisans of his vanquished rival the verdict that the victor, James R. Keene's great son of Domino, was one of the best horses that the American turf has ever produced." (May 24, 1901) Keene was one of America's greatest turfmen, entering his horses in races throughout the United States as well as in England and France. Born in England in 1838, he made his first fortune in San Francisco speculating on Comstock Lode shares in the early 1870s. Moving to New York in 1876, he was badly burned when Jay Gould sold him out of the pool they formed for a bear raid on Western Union stock. He recouped his losses in the roaring bull market of 1879, but lost nearly everything when the price of wheat collapsed from $1.30 to $0.90 in 1884. He gradually rebuilt his fortunes, and 1901 was his greatest year: he syndicated the initial public offering of United States Steel, then and for many years to come the largest offering in history.

Trophy for the 1902 running of the Belmont Stakes designed by Paulding Farnham. It was won at Morris Park on May 22 by Masterman, bred and owned by Belmont himself; Masterman was sired by Hastings, the winner of Augie Belmont's only previous Belmont Stakes victory in 1896 (see page 199). William C. Whitney's King Hanover was the favorite in the 1902 race, but Masterman shot ahead at the start and held the lead all the way to the finish, winning by two lengths over J. B. Haggin's Ranald; King Hanover was third. The trophy appears to have been seriously damaged and poorly restored, or perhaps entirely remade. Originally the wings of Victory were spread out; only the horse's right hind hoof touched the base, and his head was straight forward: the horse now appears to be about to fall forward.

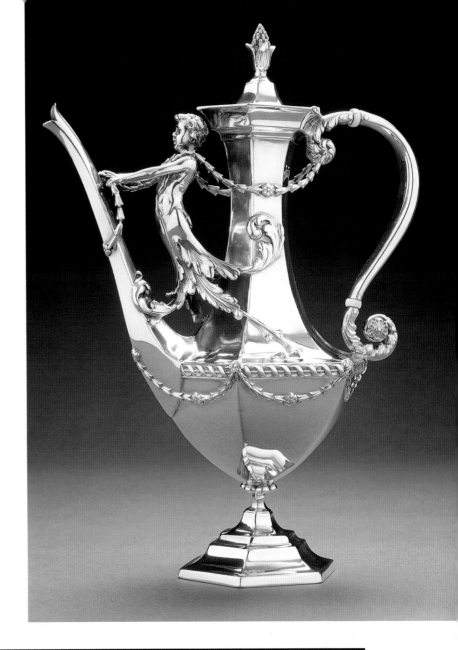

➤ Renaissance-inspired after-dinner coffeepot designed by Paulding Farnham for the 1900 Paris Exposition and shown again at the 1901 Buffalo Exhibition. Recalling the figurehead of a nineteenth-century sailing ship, a water spirit decked with acanthus holds the spout of the 10⅜-inch-tall pot, and a bellflower swag connects him with its neck. ➤

➤ Renaissance Revival centerpiece probably designed by Paulding Farnham circa 1896, with Tiffany's factory drawing in the background. The sides of the 22-inch-long oval centerpiece have chased putti and fauns dancing under a grapevine. Several versions of this piece were made; this one was given to President and Mrs. William Howard Taft by President Manuel Estrada Cabrera of Guatemala on the occasion of the Tafts' twenty-fifth (silver) wedding anniversary, June 11, 1911. Estrada Cabrera gained power in 1898 with the assassination of one of Guatemala's few legitimately elected presidents. The effort to topple his dictatorial regime threatened to engulf the whole of Central America in war, but Presidents Theodore Roosevelt and Porfirio Díaz of Mexico arranged an armistice in 1906. Estrada Cabrera was finally ousted in 1920. ➤

LOUIS COMFORT TIFFANY AND ALBERT ANGELL SOUTHWICK

ARTHUR LEROY BARNEY

✐ Byzantine-style silver box with Favrile glass insets designed by Louis Comfort Tiffany and made by Tiffany Studios circa 1905. A nearly identical box was shown by Louis Comfort Tiffany at La Société des Artistes Français in Paris in 1906. ✐

Tea set with bakelite handles and New Zealand jade finials designed for the 1939–40 World's Fair by Arthur L. Barney. Its sleek, aerodynamic styling imparts the sense of forward movement characteristic of late 1930s design.

merica's greatest figure in the history of the decorative arts, Louis Comfort Tiffany (1848–1933),
worked extensively in bronze, enameled copper,
and even enameled gold, but he showed little interest in silver.
Possibly he considered it the domain of his father, Charles
Lewis Tiffany. He would, nonetheless, exert his authority on
silver design at Tiffany & Co. following his father's death on
February 18, 1902.

The eclectic, often revivalist, tastes of James Whitehouse,
Eugene Soligny, and Paulding Farnham that had exerted
such major influence on Tiffany silver design in the later part
of the nineteenth century were totally in opposition to Louis
Comfort Tiffany's profound commitment to the Arts and Crafts
movement in general and to Art Nouveau in particular, territories in which he was a world leader. When Whitehouse and
Soligny died, only Paulding Farnham remained of the *ancien
régime*, and Louis Comfort Tiffany would waste no time in sub-
ordinating him to his own authority.

The tale of two drawings in the Tiffany Archives for
a souvenir spoon designed by Paulding Farnham reveals the
uncomfortable relationship between Tiffany and Farnham.
Tiffany's majestic new store—designed by Louis Comfort
Tiffany's friend and sometime collaborator, Stanford White—
opened on the southeast corner of Fifth Avenue and 37th Street
on September 5, 1905, immediately after the close of the 1904–5
St. Louis World's Fair and the return of the unsold exhibition
pieces to Tiffany & Co. Nine days later, Farnham submitted a
drawing for a souvenir spoon commemorating the opening. It
depicted a neo-Renaissance Atlas—not the picturesque
Victorian Atlas of Tiffany's famous clock—holding up a medallion of the new store, and all crowned by two putti making obvious reference to the figures on Farnham's vast Renaissance
Revival silver service from the St. Louis Exposition. The putti
alone were a Farnham signature; but, in case they were not
enough, Farnham stamped the drawing, not with the invariable
Tiffany & Co. silver design department's oval stamp, but with
his own, larger, shield-shaped stamp, which read "Paulding
Farnham, September 14, 1905."

Shortly after Farnham's uncle, Tiffany's president Charles
T. Cook, died on January 26, 1907, Louis Comfort Tiffany
revised the souvenir spoon project. Less than four months

Eight-inch-tall Byzantine-style three-
handled chalice with emeralds and
turquoises designed by Louis Comfort
Tiffany and made by Tiffany Studios
about 1905.

Punch bowl designed in the Beaux Arts style by Albert A. Southwick, from the 119-piece service presented by the state of New Jersey on August 14, 1907 to the U.S.S. *New Jersey*, a battleship of the United States Navy. The bowl is 22 inches tall, and its base is 32 inches long. The figures on the base represent Liberty and Prosperity.

after Cook's death, a drawing of a new version of the spoon was sent to the silver department, this time with the traditional Tiffany & Co. Atlas figure and with Farnham's putti crossed off and bearing the notation, "Leave figures off. This change was *ordered* by Mr. L. C. Tiffany on May 17, 1907." If the message was not clear enough, a second note on the new drawing read, "Design returned with thanks—Please be careful to have all future spoons made to conform to the pattern as altered by Mr. L. C. Tiffany." One year later Paulding Farnham would leave Tiffany & Co. forever.

Louis Comfort Tiffany himself designed few pieces of silver, but when the new Tiffany's opened in 1905, he had ample selections of his "Favrile" glass, his bronze objects, his Art Nouveau jewelry and his enameled wares on display. He also had a talented young silver designer well versed in the Art Nouveau style named Albert Angell Southwick (1872–1960) to aid him in his projects.

Southwick had studied first at the Rhode Island School of Design in Providence as an evening student between 1884 and 1888. Beginning in 1887 he also worked as a designer at the newly formed Sterling Company division of Howard & Son in Providence where he remained until 1893 when he decided to continue his education with the study of steel engraving at the

School of Applied Arts in Berlin. From Berlin he went on to visit Dresden and Vienna in order to further his knowledge of design and metalsmithing before entering the French national Ecole des Beaux-Arts in Paris in 1898. While in Paris, he also took courses at the Académie Julian, a private art school on the rue du Dragon not far from the Beaux-Arts.

The French capital was the world center of the Art Nouveau movement during the years Southwick studied there (1898–1900), and his designing was strongly influenced by its highly mannered, curvilinear, organic style as well as by the rather grandiose and academic style of the Beaux-Arts.

It must be noted that Southwick's father, James Mortimer Southwick (1846–1904), was a naturalist of some stature, having been the founding curator of Providence's Roger Williams Park Museum of Natural History. His devotion to natural history was undoubtedly a strong influence on his son's design direction.

"King Cole" children's mug in the Art Nouveau style designed by Albert A. Southwick circa 1905. Tiffany's made matching plates, bowls, and napkin rings. The mug was put back into production in 1982. ⟩⟩

OPPOSITE:
⟩ Designed circa 1906 by Albert A. Southwick in the Art Nouveau style, this silver-gilt coffee set is studded with citrines, and the tray is inset with panels of nephrite jade. Southwick's work was greatly admired by Gustave Stickley, leader of the Arts and Crafts movement in America. Stickley held that crafts such as silvermaking could equal the fine art of painting. He wrote in 1906: "Just now the vogue is for pictures . . . and to be a designer, to make metal or wood or pewter a means of expression for interesting thought, is less popular. And so it is interesting to find a man, an artist like Albert A. Southwick, practically giving his life to creating interesting designs and new methods in craftsmanship for commercial purposes. To be sure there are few establishments where a man would be allowed greater freedom for developing workmanship than . . . Tiffany & Company; still . . . there must be a great love and appreciation of the importance of industrial art to hold one to the artisan's table instead of the artist's easel." ("Artist and Silversmith—How One Man Worked to be a Successful Designer," *The Craftsman*, May 1906) ⟩

After viewing the great Paris Exposition of 1900, where he must have admired Tiffany's grand prize-winning displays of silverware and of jewelry, both the work of Paulding Farnham, Albert Southwick returned to Providence. There he continued his design career until he moved to New York to join Tiffany's silver design department in 1903 during preparations for the 1904 St. Louis World's Fair; Farnham was hard at work preparing the massive service of elaborately detailed Renaissance Revival silver that would be the showpiece of Tiffany's silver exhibit, an exhibit that would again win a grand prize for silver.

There is no evidence that Southwick's participation in the Tiffany silver designs in any way influenced Paulding Farnham, who was given total credit for the Tiffany & Co. silver exhibit in St. Louis. However, Southwick's proficiency in the Art Nouveau style must have attracted the attention of Louis Comfort Tiffany, who was working on Tiffany's jewelry exhibit for St. Louis when Southwick was hired. Tiffany would eventually put Southwick in charge of silver design after Farnham's departure in 1908.

In a four-page illustrated article in the May 1906 issue of *The Craftsman*, American Arts and Crafts Movement leader Gustav Stickley was the first to comment on Southwick's

Covered silver-gilt vase, made in 1909, engraved with stylized carnations with silver outer petals. The stems and the border around the base show the lingering influence of Art Nouveau. The vase belonged to Edsel Ford, son and heir of the founder of Ford Motor Company, and is now displayed at the Edsel and Eleanor Ford House in Grosse Pointe Shores, Michigan. In 1920 Tiffany & Co. purchased and exhibited a collection of early American silver assembled by George S. Palmer, a pioneer collector of American decorative arts. Tiffany's sold the Palmer collection to Edsel Ford, and it became the nucleus of Ford's silver collection.

expertise in Art Nouveau design as exhibited by his silverwares for Tiffany's:

> The latter part of Mr. Southwick's work in Europe was during the first flush of interest in the Art Nouveau movement. His work with the Tiffany Company shows this influence markedly . . . where freedom of thought is permitted there is the new art feeling, the using of simple designs in permanently beautiful effects. For instance, a noteworthy silver bowl carries a decoration of a pine branch and owl, most simply done, but the lights and shades, the relief, is so managed, so massed that there is atmosphere and mystery, almost a sense of night. It is the silversmith as an artist. A silver coffee set has no ornamentation but clusters of berry leaves, but the proportion is perfect and the ornament applied so as to intensify, not mar, the beauty of line. In other words, the composition is good, as it would be in a painting. Mr. Southwick is versatile in his craftsmanship. He again resembles the old artists in that his cultivated ability has many expressions. In half a dozen different ways he is ranked as exceptional.

Much of Southwick's design sense was firmly entrenched in the idiom of Art Nouveau, whose vocabulary was not at all incompatible with the Tiffany tradition of elaborate showpieces such as gem-ornamented coffee services. Southwick would provide designs for these, which included insets of nephrite jade and faceted citrine accents on eighteen-karat-gold demitasse sets. He would later use his Beaux-Arts training to abandon Art Nouveau altogether in his best-known masterpiece, the grandiose 119-piece silver service he designed for the U.S.S. *New Jersey,* which was made in 1906 and presented to the the crew of the old battleship by Governor Edward C. Stokes on August 14, 1907.

Southwick retained his position as head silver designer and continued to work closely with Louis Comfort Tiffany until 1919, but the production of Art Nouveau silverware was limited at Tiffany & Co., and records give few further details of Southwick's later career in Tiffany silver design. By the time of the San Francisco Panama-Pacific International Exposition of 1915, the Tiffany silver, gold, and enamel exhibition pieces shown were all credited to Louis Comfort Tiffany, although Southwick probably did the finished drawings for these pieces from Tiffany's sketches.

Sixteen-inch-tall vase designed by Albert A. Southwick circa 1907. Like the loving cup opposite, it is copper inlaid on highly polished silver, but its form and decoration are neoclassical rather than Art Nouveau. The frieze recalls early-nineteenth-century neoclassical sculpture by Bertel Thorvaldsen (1770–1844), and may reflect Southwick's training in Berlin and Paris.

Tiffany's employee ledgers record that on July 6, 1906, Albert A. Southwick was working at the Forest Hill, New Jersey, silver shop "under direction of Mr. Louis C. Tiffany," although there is no evidence that Louis Comfort himself ever had personal involvement in the New Jersey silver shop beyond sending sketches to Southwick.

Louis Tiffany's designs made in the Tiffany & Co. workshops on the sixth floor of the Thirty-seventh Street store in Manhattan or in Forest Hill were supervised by his collaborators: the jewelry by Julia Munson and the silver and enamel by Dr. Parker McIlhiney (who had focused on the composition of the enamels used on Louis Tiffany's enamel wares at Tiffany's own shop, Tiffany Studios, before he joined Tiffany & Co. Southwick undoubtedly collaborated with McIlhiney and Tiffany on the production of enameled objects until McIlhiney left Tiffany's on August 1, 1914 (shortly before the San Francisco Exposition).

Louis Tiffany himself would have little direct involvement with Tiffany & Co. after 1918 and would finally close his Tiffany Studios in 1922. Southwick relinquished his post as head silver designer to Arthur Leroy Barney in 1919 and on May 20, 1922, was transferred to Tiffany & Co.'s branch in Paris where he held the post of co-manager. Two years later he became the co-manager of Tiffany's London branch as well. He retired from Tiffany & Co. in 1951 when the company's Paris offices closed; they were not reopened until 1999, thirty-nine years after Albert Southwick's death in 1960.

To honor Southwick's memory and his contributions to Tiffany silver design, his daughters, grandchildren, and great-grandchildren were guests of honor at the December 2, 1999, opening of Tiffany's present Paris branch at 7, rue de la Paix, just across the street from the former Tiffany's that Southwick had co-managed.

✍ Art Nouveau loving cup designed by Albert A. Southwick circa 1905. Highly polished silver inlaid with copper, 6½ inches tall. ✍

Octagonal box decorated with turquoises, designed by Louis Comfort Tiffany and made by Tiffany Furnaces, his glass–manufacturing company in Corona, New York. Louis Tiffany's photo album indicates that he displayed a similar box at the 1904 St. Louis Exposition.

OPPOSITE:

Twenty-two-inch-tall covered urn designed by Louis Comfort Tiffany and Albert A. Southwick for the 1915 Panama-Pacific World Exposition in San Francisco. The Limoges enamel frieze around the top is a miniature version of two murals Louis Tiffany painted for The Briars, his Oyster Bay country house circa 1898. This side shows women and girls presenting flowers to the goddess Flora; the other side shows the goddess Ceres in her carriage with attendants carrying baskets of fruit. Directors of Bethlehem Steel presented the urn to their chairman, Charles Schwab (see page 110), on February 18, 1922. At the time, Schwab was the highest-paid executive in the United States.

Cigar box in the form of a Pueblo dwelling made in 1918 for the battleship U.S.S. *New Mexico*, whose silver service included twenty-four dessert plates engraved with scenes of New Mexican history.

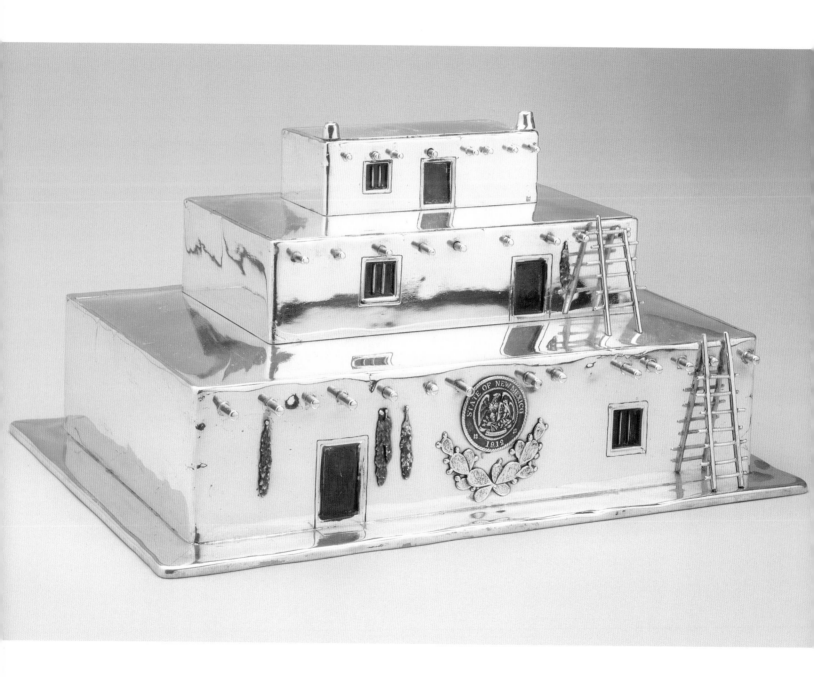

ARTHUR LEROY BARNEY

About two years after Albert Southwick came to work as a silver designer at Tiffany & Co., he was joined by another Providence, Rhode Island–born designer, Arthur Leroy Barney (1884–1955).

Although he was twelve years Southwick's junior, the two must have had some connection through their Providence backgrounds. Both had studied at the Rhode Island School of Design; Barney was an evening student from fall 1899 to spring 1904 (by day he was an apprentice at Gorham from October 1900). In any case, Barney came to Tiffany as a silver designer in 1906, possibly to collaborate with Southwick on the U.S.S *New Jersey* silverware. Pay records at Tiffany & Co. would indicate that following Dr. Parker McIlhiney's retirement on August 1, 1914, Barney's responsibilities in the silver shop under Southwick increased significantly. He was so successful that when Louis Comfort Tiffany and Southwick withdrew from Tiffany silver, Barney became head silver designer in 1919, a position he retained until shortly before his death in 1955. In 1937 he was also made vice president, assistant treasurer and director of Tiffany & Co.

In 1933, at the height of the Great Depression, Barney created a remarkable solid platinum after-dinner coffee service shown at the 1933–34 Century of Progress International Exposition in Chicago. The service, comprising a tray, coffeepot, creamer, sugar bowl, and tongs, weighed 112 troy ounces and was the only hollowware shown by Tiffany & Co. at that time when the ravaged economy had eliminated all demand for silver hollowware. Neither Barney nor Tiffany & Co. had any hope of selling this unique platinum service. It did make an attention-getting showpiece; and, after the Chicago Exposition, the platinum was put to practical use in the mountings of diamonds and sapphires.

Though the Depression was far from over in 1937, that year Barney designed the American Art Deco flatsilver pattern "Century" to commemorate Tiffany & Co.'s centennial. The few hollowware pieces (low, angular four-light candelabra and square service plates) that Barney designed to complement the flatware were modest for all their pared-down Art Deco

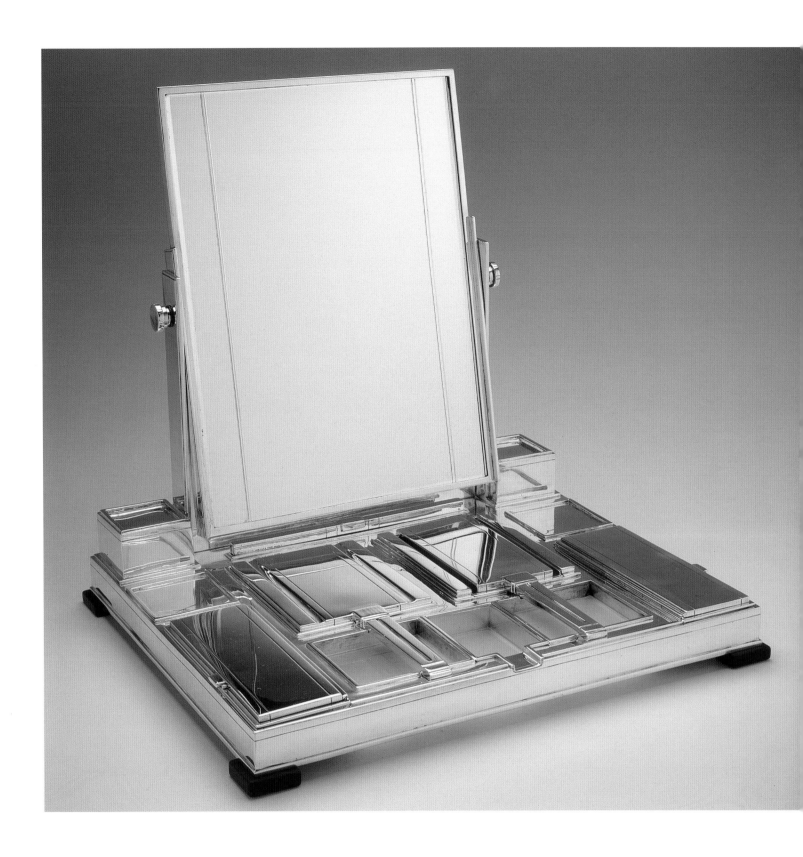

The crisp rectangles of this vanity case designed by Arthur L. Barney in 1936 are characteristic of mid-1930s Art Deco.

sleekness and stylishness.

Barney's designing talents would only fully come into their own two years later in the magnificent display of Tiffany American Deco–style silver designed for the New York World's Fair of 1939–40 and shown there in the exposition's pavillion of jewels and silver, House of Jewels.

Silver design, however, was not to be a focus of the 1940s. By the time of the New York World's Fair, the world still had in no way recovered from the Great Depression, and was sinking deeper into World War II. The jewels and silver displayed by Tiffany & Co. in the fair's House of Jewels would almost all be returned. It was displayed in Tiffany's new American Deco–style store at the corner of Fifty-seventh Street and Fifth Avenue; and some of the items, such as Barney's extravagant eighteen-karat-gold jewelry box, would appear in Tiffany catalogues into the 1950s.

Arthur L. Barney was a designer of great imagination and talent who created the American Deco style's most remarkable works in silver. He unfortunately oversaw Tiffany design in the worst decades of our country's economic history, when so little was possible as far as luxury goods such as silverware were concerned.

The styles of the 1939 World's Fair, including Barney's wonderful silver pieces, although highly sought after today, quickly fell from grace and were so little appreciated that they came to be known as Retro Modern. There was, however, nothing "retro" about them, and Barney's extraordinary designs for Tiffany's 1939 display had, with one giant step, brought Tiffany silver into the Age of Transportation and the "World of Tomorrow" with all the cool, sleek, and debonair elegance of those times.

The last important commission designed by Barney was for forty-nine additional pieces of silver to be added to the U.S.S. *New Jersey* service in 1952 which was, of course, in the style of his former boss, Albert A. Southwick. He retired in April 1955.

On the day after Barney died, the *New York Herald Tribune* accurately—but tersely—noted on November 9, 1955, that, "He was internationally known for his work in designing Tiffany's line of silverware."

Tiffany's silver display case in the House of Jewels at the 1939–40 New York World's Fair. Most pieces in the case are illustrated in the following pages. This display was much smaller than Tiffany's displays at the great expositions in the late nineteenth and early twentieth centuries, reflecting the waning of interest in important silver due to the Great Depression.

Centerpiece and matching candelabra designed by Arthur L. Barney for the 1939–40 New York World's Fair, where the centerpiece was priced at $1,850 and the candelabra at $1,250. The ensemble sold at Christie's on June 6, 1992 for $55,000.

Eighteen-karat-gold jewelry box designed by Arthur L. Barney for the 1939–40 New York World's Fair, where it was priced at $2,000. It evidently failed to sell, for it reappeared twelve years later in Tiffany's 1951 Christmas catalogue priced at $5,300.

Designed by Arthur L. Barney for the 1939–40 World's Fair, this cocktail set was embellished with pale cabochon emeralds. The shaker, representing a lighthouse, was priced at $500, the eight cups at $720, and the tray at $480.

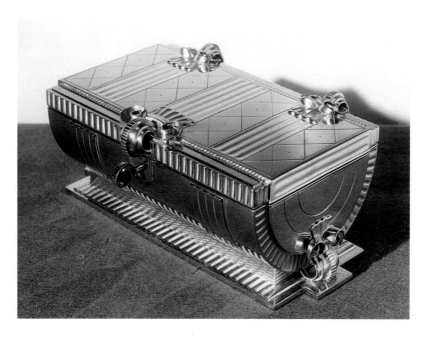

Eighteen-karat-gold jewelry box, 8 inches long, designed by Arthur L. Barney for the 1939–40 New York World's Fair. Tiffany's 1939 caption for this photo reads, "In the form of half a cylinder, the curved side of which rests on a fluted base, and is supported at each end by modern wrought scroll and shell ornaments. These ornaments are repeated on the flat cover to form the hinge bearers and lock clasp. The body and cover have concave and convex fluted borders and panels and the cover has a series of large engraved lozenges." It was priced at $4,000.

✍ Centerpiece bowl, 11¾ inches in diameter, designed by Arthur L. Barney and made in 1940 for the 1939–40 New York World's Fair. Tiffany's 1940 photograph caption reads, "This bowl has 27 concave flutes and stands on a circular base and is supported by 9 arms between which are wrought, ribbon-like ornaments." It was priced at $1,600. ✍

✍ Archival photograph of a coffee set designed circa 1939 under the direction of Arthur L. Barney. The lids and the center of the tray are chased with stylized coffee leaves and berries. ✍

LEFT:
Five-light "American Deco" candelabrum with scrolls and stylized leaf motifs designed by Charles B. Blake for the 1939–40 World's Fair and completed in 1940.

BELOW:
The matching centerpiece, with its openwork top, was intended for flower arrangements.

OPPOSITE, BELOW:
Designed by Oscar Riedener circa 1950, this 11-inch-tall pitcher's unusual shape and martelé surface give it a handmade quality characteristic of the Arts and Crafts movement at the turn of the century.

"American Moderne" pinecone centerpiece and matching candelabra designed by Oscar Riedener (1901–2000) in 1949. Riedener joined Tiffany's in 1926, working in the silver design department under Arthur Barney, whom he assisted with the silver made for the 1939–40 New York World's Fair. In the late 1940s he produced admirable pieces of his own. His work, influenced by Scandinavian design as well as French Art Deco, was more graceful than Barney's, which has purely American Deco geometric forms and uncompromisingly flat planes of high-polished silver played off against scrolls and undulations of more flat polished sheets of silver. Riedener's work has fluid tapering and curving lines, and characteristically has softer—sometimes even hammered—surfaces that approach the look of Tiffany's Arts and Crafts style "special handwork." Riedener briefly succeeded Barney as head of silver design in 1955, but after Walter Hoving appointed Van Day Truex as Tiffany's design director, Riedener focused most of his career on Tiffany's advertising, eventually becoming the vice president in charge of the department. He retired after sixty-two years at Tiffany's on January 1, 1989.

VAN DAY TRUEX

FRANK LLOYD WRIGHT

ELSA PERETTI

⚉ Left: silver-gilt "Indian corn" bowl made in 1981 from electro-forming patterns used in 1877 to make four silver-plated replicas of the Bryant Vase (see page 92). Right: designed by John Loring in 1981, these candleholders were made from casting patterns taken from actual crabs and sea urchins. They were inspired by bronze and Favrile glass crab inkwells designed by Louis Comfort Tiffany circa 1915 and sold with other desk accessories at Tiffany & Co.'s store on Fifth Avenue at Thirty-seventh Street. ⚉

_ Designed by John Loring in 1980, the surface of
the 10½-inch-long box is based on the "tread-plate"
pattern applied with roller dies to aluminum and
steel flooring to prevent skidding. The box was not
chased with the traditional hammers or dies, but with
a more recent process that uses compressed air to
chase the low-relief pattern. _

Tiffany design changed dramatically from the American Deco and 1940s styles of Arthur L. Barney in 1955 when the company's new owner, Walter Hoving, appointed Van Day Truex (1904–1979) as design director of Tiffany & Co.

Truex had been at the Parsons School of Design Paris branch from 1925, the year of the great Paris "Art Deco" Exposition, to the outbreak of World War II in 1939, first as a student and then as a teacher, and finally as the school's director. He was president of the school in New York from 1942 to 1953. He continued throughout his lifetime to maintain close ties with France and French design; and, for his efforts following World War II in promoting French products and in revitalizing the design of French luxury goods, the French government made him a chevalier of the Legion of Honor in 1951, four years before he joined Tiffany & Co.

Although Truex had a lifelong love affair with France and French design, he had no sympathy with French Art Deco and even less with American Deco design. Van Day Truex was not at all intrigued by the lush surfaces and exaggerated forms of the French Art Deco style of the 1920s and 1930s, nor by its streamlined American counterpart; he was equally unmoved by the glittering starkness of the emerging International Modern movement. He felt Art Deco was "pointlessly grasping at the retreating shadows of eighteenth-century opulence, and the International Modernist architects and designers were trying too hard to be utilitarian and 'original.'" Truex believed that to develop appropriate design vocabulary of fine quality it was necessary to remain "aloof" from trends and to become acutely aware of the whole rich texture of civilization—its past, its present and its possible future. If the collections of the Musée des Arts Décoratifs were well known to him, so were the ideas of his friends, such as Christian Bérard, Jean-Michel Frank, Elsa Schiaparelli, and Coco Chanel. "It was all there," he would recall, "the provocative, the intellectual, the brilliant, the creative."

He was on the side of design that made a simple, direct, and honest statement and that made it with evident style, vitality, and boldness. He was as totally opposed to all that was bland, timid, and faceless as he was to sentimentality and gratuitous contrivance in design.

Tiffany Design Director Van Day Truex based his 11¼-inch-tall "Seed Pod" centerpiece, circa 1969, on Karl Blossfeldt's 1920s photograph of the fruit of *Blumenbachia hieronymi*, a rare Argentinean loasa. Truex studied art in Paris when the surrealists were fascinated by Blossfeldt's photographs of unusual plant forms. Here Truex's centerpiece is placed in front of Blossfeldt's photograph.

Truex's favored source of inspiration was nature, and he borrowed liberally not only her fruits and flowers, her leaves and plants and seeds and seed pods, but the pure abstract compositions of her structures—honeycombs, fish scales, crystals—and her natural earth colours. "Not original motifs," he said, "but Mother Nature's simply waiting to be used in another way."

Truex was not one to innovate for the sake of innovation; rather, he distilled and edited from "the vast, unlimited sources of inspiration" he saw around him, all that had a timeless purity and perfection of form and patterning and all that he saw as useful to the twentieth century.

He is remembered today in silver design first for his International Design Award–winning "Bamboo" flatsilver, introduced in 1961. However, his more interesting works in silver were his splendid centerpieces, one in the form of an airy latticework Oriental pagoda, others in the leaf and fruit forms of giant seed pods or silver pumpkins, squashes, and cabbages. "Mother Nature is the best designer" was a Van Day Truex motto, and he wittily translated nature's forms into eminently stylish pieces of Tiffany silver, or *objects*, as he preferred to call them.

Frank Lloyd Wright (1867–1959) was not only the greatest figure in the history of American architecture, he was also a world leader in the decorative arts, where his love of angularity and flat vertical planes played off against more linear horizontals had a profound and far-reaching influence on twentieth-century design.

He designed not only the furniture but also the table furnishings for his major public commissions, such as Chicago's Midway Gardens (1913) and Tokyo's Imperial Hotel (1916–20). Much of his silver hollowware design was, however, unrealized, probably because its polygonal forms, all sharp angles and flat planes, presented almost insurmountable difficulties in production.

In 1985 an agreement between Tiffany & Co. and the Frank Lloyd Wright Foundation allowed a reassessment of Wright's work in silver design, and a sizable collection of Wright silver hollowware, the greater part of it designed about 1918 for the Imperial Hotel in Tokyo, was put into production for the first time.

Wright curiously had left his designs for silver, as he had left many of his designs for glass and ceramics, unfinished. His intention and direction was in every case clear. His conclusions, although they could be drawn with mathematical certainty, were often simply not there in the drawings. Lines as well as whole perspectives were missing, and junctions were incompletely or ambiguously indicated. In the mind of this protean thinker and visionary, it must have all been so crystal clear; to lesser beings, it was often a puzzle—even if a puzzle with only one inevitable solution. From this incompleteness it was clear that the pieces had never been realized. Wright certainly knew how difficult it would be to eventually make them and decided to leave it to silversmiths of the future with more advanced technology to complete his remarkable projects for silver.

He had done this for other mediums. A striking example of this was a drawing for a tapered and footed hexagonal candle holder in crystal that was technically impossible to make at the time Wright drew it. Like the silver drawings, it was filed for future generations to produce—if they could—the perfect and impossible object in crystal. As Wright would have wanted it, the modern technologies of injection molding and acid polishing ultimately allowed Tiffany's to

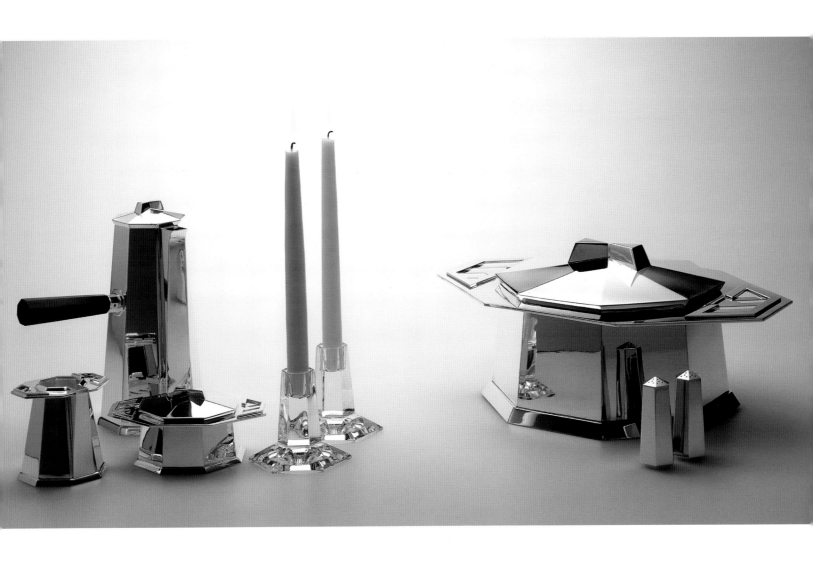

Tureen centerpiece, salt and pepper shakers, and coffee set designed circa 1918 by Frank Lloyd Wright for the Imperial Hotel in Tokyo. These designs were not executed until 1985, when Tiffany & Co. produced them under an agreement with the Frank Lloyd Wright Foundation. The sleek, elegant, complex objects show that the Art Deco movement was influenced by Wright's work, often called "rectilinear Art Nouveau." They also remind us that Wright's genius ranged well beyond architecture: he occasionally pointed out that the spiral form of the Guggenheim Museum in New York was based on his (never-executed) design for a salad bowl.

realize this ideal crystal candle holder in 1985, just as Tiffany's silversmiths finally realized Frank Lloyd Wright 's silver designs. Both were of the same family, favoring tapering hexagonal forms and demanding a nearly impossible precision in their crafting.

Despite their splendid simplicity, clarity, and perfection of geometric form, the high level of craftsmanship required to execute Wright's designs brought them to the market at relatively high prices, seriously restricting the number of pieces that were eventually produced. The project was ended in June 2000, but the superb and imaginative Frank Lloyd Wright silverware produced by Tiffany's over a fifteen-year period merits its place in the history of American silver design.

Designed by artist Eric Erickson in the 1990s these electroformed pitchers are based on Ohio art pottery prototypes of the 1940s.

Loving cup designed by architect Michael Graves in the 1980s as a homage to silverware produced early in the twentieth century by the Wiener Werkstätte designers Josef Hoffmann and Dagobert Peche.

In 1974 a young Italian woman of genius, who was to become the most successful and celebrated jewelry designer of the late twentieth century, came to Tiffany & Co., where she singlehandedly brought silver jewelry back into fashion.

Elsa Peretti began her design career while working as a high-fashion model in the early 1970s. Her first designs were silver accessories that she created to be worn with the clothes of her friend, the New York star fashion designer of the 1960s and 1970s, Halston. Amongst these was her eminently stylish, large-scale, silver "Equestrian Buckle," which became an icon of 1970s fashion.

The silver accessories that Peretti first created for Halston were so successful that, by 1974, she decided to devote her talents exclusively to jewelry design, and later to jewel-like accessories for the home. Today the designs of Elsa Peretti, with their smooth, sensual, undulated surfaces and their deceptively simple, organic, abstract forms are world famous. The Peretti "Open Heart," "Bean," "Teardrop," "Bone Cuff," and "Equestrian Buckle" are all icons of late-twentieth-century jewelry, admired and worn throughout the world.

Peretti's aesthetic sensibilities are a perfect fit with Tiffany's. Like Edward C. Moore, she is a devoted admirer of Japanese craftsmanship and design and a collector of Chinese and Japanese furniture and art. She surrounds herself with such objects in her daily life; their refinement of form and consummate handling of materials inspire her. Peretti has also sought out the greatest craftsmen of China and Japan to participate in the production of her designs; and, like Edward C. Moore, Louis Comfort Tiffany, and Van Day Truex, she is a student and lover of nature whose forms she has abstracted and refined into objects of sheer perfection.

In 1978 and 1979 Peretti turned her formidable skills to silver hollowware design with a small collection that included an eleven-and-a-half-inch tray with her signature indented thumbprints as handles, a pumpkin bowl with a black oxidized silver cover sporting a handwoven black silk braid and tassel as a handle, a sculptural fifteen-inch silver "Bone" candlestick, and another smaller-scaled candlestick, unexpectedly asymmetrical and supine. All her silver hollowware designs, like her silver jewelry, are seductively tactile.

Hiro's surrealistic photograph of water leaping with a gravity-defying will of its own from Elsa Peretti's organically formed pitcher.

Tureen with lid and tray designed by Elsa Peretti in 1986 and made by the Pampaloni Company in Florence. The tureen is 13½ inches in diameter and 7 inches high.

In 1984 Peretti's innovative "Padova" flatsilver was introduced, along with her amply scaled, volumetric, and subtly sculpted silver tureen centerpiece (which evolved from her pumpkin bowl) and her equally subtle and surprisingly sensual silver water pitcher with its asymmetrical handle recalling her horizontal candlestick.

In their total departure from all traditional silver design, Peretti's works are unique. As with the volumetric, asymmetrical, and organic forms of the best of Louis Comfort Tiffany's "Favrile" designs in the field of glassware, Peretti's designs march into territories so completely unexplored by silversmiths before her that her work is truly revolutionary. However, unlike "Favrile" glass, which depended on the originality of its molten forms as well as on its richly textured and colored iridescent surfaces, Peretti's at once simple and astonishing silver designs depend only on a superb refinement of nature's organic forms coupled with an unerring eye for sensuality, and finally on the pure unadorned beauty of polished silver.

CHAPTER 6:
INTO THE TWENTY-FIRST CENTURY

∽ Flanked by NBC's Greg Gumbel and Denver Broncos coach Mike Shanahan, Broncos quarterback John Elway raises the Vince Lombardi Super Bowl Trophy after the Broncos defeated the Green Bay Packers by 31–24 to win Super Bowl XXXII on January 25, 1998 at the Qualcomm Stadium in San Diego. Designed by Oscar Riedener, the trophy was first presented to the Green Bay Packers for their Super Bowl I victory in 1967. In 1970 it was renamed for the late Vince Lombardi to commemorate the coach who led Green Bay to victories in Super Bowls I and II. ∽

∽ Tiger Woods holding the Mercedes Championship Trophy after winning his fifth straight Professional Golf Association tour victory in the $522,000 Mercedes Championship, played January 6–9, 2000 in Kapalua, Hawaii. Woods went on to win the "Grand Slam"— all four major tournaments in a row: the U.S. Open on June 18, the British Open on July 23, the PGA Championship on August 20, and the Masters on April 8, 2001. ∽

Edward C. Moore's Tiffany School virtually revolutionized the history of silver with its thoroughly American vision and underlying premise of nature as the original source of all design. This vision was enriched by his more personal penchant for turning away from English and continental European design vocabularies to take inspiration from the elegant abstractions of nature found in Japanese and Islamic art. Through this, Moore set Tiffany silver on the path to its continuing evolution of a vigorous, uncomplicated, original, and universally appealing style that is uniquely American.

Of course, the lessons learned from Asia and from the Islamic world are visible in Moore's Tiffany silver in the pattern and surface ornament that is essentially two-dimensional, in the fondness for asymmetry, and in the accent on form rather than on surface decoration. However, beyond that, Moore's Japanesque silver no more resembles Japanese prototypes than an Edouard Manet Impressionist painting resembles the Japanese woodblock prints that inspired it; and, his Saracenic silver no more resembles Islamic art than Orientalist paintings by John Frederick Lewis resemble the Persian miniatures that inspired them.

Both Moore's Japanesque and Saracenic styles in silver took inspiration (as did Manet and Lewis) from the arts of foreign civilization, but Moore's styles transformed those inspirations into shining examples of America's ongoing love affair with the unspoiled natural beauty of the American continents and their flora and fauna. How opposite Moore's direction was from Europe's seemingly endless following of the elaborately ornamented Rococo silver design styles of the great early-eighteenth-century French master Thomas Germain (1673–1748), or of the great neoclassical English silversmith Paul Storr (1771–1844).

This evolution of a truly American style in silver that Moore set in motion continued, as did the American art it closely paralleled, in its determination to turn its back on academic realism and lead on toward greater and greater abstraction. The overall patterns of repeated natural forms of John T. Curran and the stark, bold Native American pictograms of Paulding Farnham used to such spectacular advantage on Tiffany silver followed in the footsteps of Moore's Japanesque and Saracenic wares, further simplifying and abstracting nature.

This refining and simplifying design process would be carried on by the pure crystalline forms of Arthur Barney and Frank Lloyd Wright; then by the stylish magnifications of the

Cynthia Cooper of the Houston Comets holding the Women's National Basketball Association Championship trophy after the Comets won Game 2 of the WNBA finals at Houston's Compaq Center on November 28, 2000. The Comets beat New York's Liberty 79–73 in overtime, continuing their position as the WNBA's only champions: they have won all four WNBA finals since they began in 1997. Cooper, the Association's MVP for four straight years, retired after the 2000 finals: thirty-seven years old, she turned in an outstanding performance in the last game of her career. The trophy, created in 1997, has a 7-inch WNBA basketball atop three columns set at an angle into a curved triangular base.

curious details of nature of Van Day Truex's seed pods and by the polished sensuality of Elsa Peretti's organic gourdlike forms—descendants of Edward C. Moore's Japanesque gourd-like forms, but further abstracted by their completely unadorned, brightly polished surfaces.

Tiffany's "Tread Plate" silver of the 1980s is a direct, if greatly abstracted, descendant of Edward C. Moore's "Japanesque" rice patterns of the 1870s. Michael Graves's hammered-surface loving cup—also of the 1980s—is a descendant of Moore's hammered surfaces on his Japanesque silver; and the spiral form of Tiffany's 1990s silver pitcher inspired by Ohio art pottery is a modernization of Charles Osborne's organic spiral forms of the 1880s.

Today the ultimate abstraction and simplification of Tiffany silver is carried on in the sleek and futuristic trophies that are powerful symbols of American sports. Since producing its first important sporting trophies in the late 1850s and early 1860s, such as the Woodlawn Cup of 1861 (now the perpetual trophy for the Preakness Stakes), Tiffany & Co. has remained for nearly 150 years the world's premier source of sporting trophies. The tradition continues to this day with the world-famous Vince Lombardi Super Bowl trophy for football, the National Basketball Association Championship trophy, and baseball's World Series Cup.

From the Gilded Age of the yachting and horse racing trophies of Ogden Goelet, James Gordon Bennett, and August Belmont right on up to the golden age of American sports represented by Michael Jordan, John Elway, and Tiger Woods, Tiffany & Co. has been there designing and crafting the magnificent silver objects that commemorate extraordinary achievement in all fields of sport.

The detailed, elaborate, and iconographically rich trophies of James H. Whitehouse and Eugene Soligny, Charles Osborne's sailing trophies awash with silver mermaids and tritons swimming amongst golden seaweed, pearls, assorted seahorses, and seashells, and the vigorous horse-racing trophies of Paulding Farnham have given way in the twentieth century to more suave and streamlined geometric, brightly polished forms, which include, of course, footballs, basketballs, baseballs, tennis and golf balls, and other assorted globes joined by the occasional racehorse or yacht.

Out of the celebrated and richly textured history of sporting trophies preserved at race courses, yacht clubs, country clubs, sports associations, and museums across

America has come a new generation of icons of American sports, whose role occupies a unique place in the imagination of sports fans as fabled symbols of aspiration and achievement. And that is the role of magnificent Tiffany silver in the future—just as it was its role in the past—to symbolize aspiration and achievement.

New York Yankees owner George Steinbrenner, Mayor Rudolf Giuliani, and Yankees manager Joe Torre with the World Series Trophy at City Hall on October 31, 2000 during the celebration of the Yankees' "Subway Series" victory over the New York Mets. The 2-foot-tall trophy was created in 2000. The thirty flags represent all the major-league teams; the dome's latitude and longitude lines represent the world and its silver-gilt "stitches" represent a baseball. Officially known as "The Commissioner's Trophy," additional examples will be made each year for the Baseball Commissioner's presentation to future World Series winners.

Chris Henderson of the Kansas City Wizards holding the Alan I. Rothenberg Trophy for Major League Soccer after the Wizards defeated the Chicago Fire 1–0 at the Robert F. Kennedy Stadium in Washington, D.C. on October 15, 2000. It was the Wizards' first championship and the fifth year of the League championship.

Michael Jordan of the Chicago Bulls holding the Larry O'Brien NBA Championship Trophy after the Bulls won the fifth and final game of the National Basketball Association's 1991 playoffs at the Great Western Forum in Los Angeles. It was the Bulls' first victory in the NBA finals: minutes later a tearful Jordan told the press, "It's been a long, long seven years. A lot of bad teams, a lot of improvement . . . I told people, if we got to the finals we'd win. I really believed it. We shocked a lot of people, I know, but we earned it. We deserved it. We took it— no one gave it to us. That's what I'm proudest about. We took it, and we took it as a team. Me and my teammates." Jordan, voted the NBA's Most Valuable Player during the season, was the unanimous choice of the eleven-member panel as Finals MVP. Created in 1978, the 2-foot-tall trophy features a regulation-size silver and silver-gilt basketball. In 1984 it was renamed for the late Larry O'Brien, the NBA's commissioner from 1975 to 1984.

Byron Nelson and Ernie Els holding the winner's trophy after Els won the 1995 GTE Byron Nelson Classic golf tournament at Cottonwood Valley, Texas. Now called the Verizon Byron Nelson Classic, the tournament traces its origins to Nelson's winning the Texas Victory Open in 1944. Els's performance in 1995 set two records for the tournament: best score of 263 and best individual game score of 61.

Throughout Tiffany & Co.'s 150-year history of silversmithing, it was not the company's policy to have individual designers sign their works, or even sign their drawings, for that matter. However, the great degree of stylistic individualism encouraged by Edward C. Moore in the Tiffany School coupled with the vast and comprehensive collection of silver design drawings and studies for ornamental motifs preserved in the Tiffany Archives have allowed us, for the first time, to justly and accurately credit Tiffany's greatest silver designers with their master works. This task was made slightly easier by the infrequent but revealing attributions the company allowed to be made by the contemporary press over the years.

Beyond that, in our research, we were fortunate in identifying handwriting samples of most of Tiffany's leading designers and in matching them to the handwriting on their drawings. This allowed us, for example, to identify with complete certainty the important body of work by Charles Osborne, which, despite its stylistic strength, has passed through history unattributed until now. Likewise, we are able to credit John T. Curran, the designer of the celebrated Magnolia Vase in the collection of the Metropolitan Museum of Art, with many of his other remarkable works in enameled silver.

Eugene Soligny's sketchbooks in the Tiffany Archives made the task of identifying his so finely chased silver a relatively simple matter; and, beyond that, his notes and sketches spelled out his close and lifelong collaboration with James Horton Whitehouse on so many of America's great trophies. However, some other designers were more elusive. We were unable to identify with certainty any drawings of Charles T. Grosjean and have, in his case, had to rely on style alone or on U.S. patents in our attributions. In contrast, Paulding Farnham's designs are well documented in photographs preserved in either the Tiffany Archives or still in the possession of his descendents.

There is no doubt that many pieces of silver included in this book are the result of the collaboration of Edward C. Moore with one or more of the other designers working under his direction, so we have again relied on clear shifts in stylistic direction to attribute a number of Moore's Japanesque pieces to a collaboration with Charles Osborne, which began in

1879, and to attribute his later elaborately enameled Saracenic pieces to a collaboration with John T. Curran. (The latter case was quite clear cut as the overall drawings for these pieces are by Moore and the enameling patterns by Curran.)

With the exception of the Mackay silver and its antecedents, we have avoided the inclusion of pieces that were the product of complex team efforts, therefore making it impossible to attribute them to specific designers. Rather, we have focused our efforts in the desire to present the clearest possible portrait of each Tiffany master silver designer on works that exhibit the expression of a personal style.

The tasks of attribution were at times ambitious, yet we are confident that, in our enthusiasm for shedding light on and giving credit to these remarkable figures in the history of the American decorative arts, in no case have we overstepped the boundaries of verbal and visual fact and ventured into the field of unsupported conjecture.

Drawing by Edward C. Moore for Japanesque silver circa 1876.

INDEX

Page numbers in *italics* refer to illustrations.

Collection Credits

Allentown Art Museum: **235**, Gift of Bethlehem Steel Co., 1985 (1985.025.000 a,b)

The Art Institute of Chicago: **124 bottom, 125**, Gift of the Antiquarian Society through Mr. and Mrs. William Y. Hutchinson Fund (1985.221a–c); **169**, Restricted gift of Mr. and Mrs. William B. McIlvaine, Jr., (1983.18); **176 left**, Restricted gift of Mr. and Mrs. James W. Alsdorf, Mrs. Lester Armour, Mrs. George B. Young, and an anonymous donor (1978.142); **214**, Restricted Gift of Mrs. Harold T. Martin (1978.442); **247 bottom**, The Orbit Fund (199.292). All ©2000 The Art Institute of Chicago, All Rights Reserved

Autry Museum of Western Heritage, Los Angeles: **103**

John P. Axelrod Collection: **241**, courtesy Museum of Fine Arts, Boston

© Bettmann/CORBIS: **117 bottom**

© 2001 Karl Blossfeldt Archiv / Ann u. Jürgen Wilde, Köln / Artists Rights Society (ARS), NY: **251 background**

British Museum: **219 left**

Brooklyn Museum of Art: **19**, H. Randolph Lever Fund (1995.98.2); **28**, H. Randolph Lever Fund (82.18); **46 top**, (L1998.10.1.2.3a–b); **160**, (L87.9); **177 bottom**, (L1998.10.5); **191 bottom**, Courtesy George W. and Martha S. Cherkis (L86.7.3); **206**, Alfred T. and Caroline S. Zoebisch Fund (71.97); **215**, Currently on loan by Gwenna A. Miller (L83.13); **217**, Modernism Benefit Fund (87.182)

Buffalo & Erie County Historical Society, library and archives: **128**, plate 47 from *Art, Industry and Manufactures of the American Centennial Exhibition 1876*

Carnegie Museum of Art, Pittsburgh: **52 top**, DuPuy Fund; **193 right**, AODA Purchase Fund

Christie's Images: **13, 23, 70, 94, 129, 140 bottom, 144 top, 167, 190, 203, 208 top, 212 top, 243 bottom, 247 top**

Cincinnati Art Museum: **97 right**, Bequest of Reuben R. Springer (1884.483); **174 top**, source unknown (x1939.76); **208 top**, Museum purchase, Lawrence Archer Wachs Trust (2001.16)

The Cleveland Museum of Art: **42 top**, © The Cleveland Museum of Art, 2000, Norman O. Stone and Sheila A. Stone Memorial Fund, (1975.114.1–3)

Dallas Museum of Art: **43**, Gift of Tiffany & Co.; **58**, Gift of the Friends of the Decorative Arts; **63**, gift of Mr. and Mrs. Jay Gillette by exchange, Maria and John Houser Chiles, Mr. and Mrs. D.A. Berg, and Dr. and Mrs. Kenneth M. Hamlett, Jr. (1990.186)

The Diocese of New York of the Episcopal Church: **97 left**

The Doris Duke Charitable Foundation: **130–31**

Mr. and Mrs. Sean Egan: **152–53**

Ferguson Family, Fishers Island, New York: **68**

© Edsel & Eleanor Ford House, Grosse Pointe Shores, Michigan: **233**

Sir William Gladstone: **86 top**

Glasgow Museums and Art Galleries, Glasgow, Scotland: **239**

©Hearst Castle™ / California State Parks: **180–81**

High Museum of Art, Atlanta, Georgia: **213**, Virginia Carroll Crawford Collection (1984.170)

Homeland Foundation, Incorporated, New York: **88**

Mrs. Lester Kalt: **251, tureen**

Kunstgewerbemuseum, Berlin: **189**

Lauren Stanley Gallery, New York: **123 top**

Collection John Loring: **224**

Los Angeles County Museum of Art: **20–21**, Purchased with general acquisition funds and funds provided by Mr. and Mrs. Arthur Gilbert (M.85.41)

Macculloch Hall Historical Museum, Morristown, NJ: **134 left**

Major League Baseball: **262 top**. Trademarks and copyrights are used with the permission of Major League Baseball Properties, Inc.

Warren McLaughlin: **266**

Manney Collection: **212 top**

The Maryland Historical Society, Baltimore, Maryland: **77**

MetLife Archives: **237**

Metropolitan Museum of Art: **1, 92**, gift of William Cullen Bryant, 1877 (77.9ab), photograph © 1989; **65 top**, gift of a friend of the Museum, 1897 (97.1.1–.4), photograph © 1987; **79**, Gift of Cyrus W. Field, 1892 (92.10.7), photograph © 1986; **85**, Gift of Mrs. Thomas Nast, 1907 (07.273.1), photograph © 1986; **185**, Gift of Mrs.Winthrop Atwill, 1899 (99.2), photograph © 1980; **201**, Gift of Edward D. Adams, 1904 (04.1), photograph © 1989; **202**, Edgar J. Kaufmann Charitable Foundation Fund, 1969 (69.4), photograph © 1981; **226 top**, The Edgar J. Kaufmann Foundation Gift, 1969 (69.36), photograph © 1998; **246 bottom**, Gift of Erving and Joyce Wolf Foundation, 1988 (1988.200), photograph © 1999

The Minneapolis Institute of the Arts: **135, 225**

The Charles Hosmer Morse Museum of American Art, Winter Park, Florida: **49**, © The Charles Hosmer Morse Foundation, Inc.

Musée Bartholdi, Colmar, France: **99**

Museum of the City of New York: **141, 176 top right, 220**

Museum of Fine Arts, Boston: **62**, Gift of Gideon F. T. Reed (77.61); **86 top; 127 top; 187 right; 215; 218 top; 228; 241**, John P. Axelrod Collection

Museum of Fine Arts, Houston: **2**, Museum purchase with funds provided by the Agnes Cullen Arnold Fund; **106 bottom; 123 bottom, 162**, Museum purchase with funds provided by the Museum Collectors

Museum of New Mexico, Palace of the Governors: **236**

Museum of Yachting, Newport, Rhode Island: **239**, *Shamrock*, background

The National Museum of American History, Smithsonian Institution, **107**

National Museum of Racing and Hall of Fame, Saratoga Springs, New York: **222**

Department of the Navy, on loan to the New Jersey State Museum: **226 bottom**

Nelson & Nelson, New York: **102**

The Newark Museum / Art Resource, NY: **132 top left, 207, 246 top, 255**

New Jersey State Museum Collection, Trenton: **98, 192 top, 218 bottom**, Museum Purchase

© The New-York Historical Society: **53 right**, Gift from Mr. Robert G. Goelet (1982.63); **59 top**, (1983.20); **64**, (1983.9ab); **80 top**, *Frank Leslie's Illustrated Newspaper*, June 4, 1859; **159**, (73859); **172 bottom**, (73861); **176 top right** (#N1.C77).

New York Public Library: **86 bottom, 118**

New York Racing Association, Inc.: **199**

New York Yacht Club: **cover, 87, 90–91, 105, 115, 156, 165**

Anka and Cal Palitz: **188, 218 top**

Philadelphia Museum of Art: **60 top**, Given by the Friends of the Philadelphia Museum of Art

Porcellian Club: **151**

Preservation Society of Newport County: **7**

Private collection, courtesy Tim Gleason Gallery, New York: **211**

Private collection, courtesy Historical Design, Inc., New York: **194**

Private collection, courtesy Michael Weller / Argentum, San Francisco: **30; 34; 40 right; 42 bottom; 51**

Private collections: **10; 15; 27; 35 top; 46 bottom; 50** (photo Sotheby's); **67; 72 top; 111; 133; 148 left; 149; 161; 166; 172 top; 178; 187, Bat Vase; 209**, courtesy the Detroit Institute of the Arts (photo Sotheby's); **212 bottom; 232; 249**

Royal Collection, The Hague, The Netherlands: **96**

Seattle Art Museum, Ruth J. Nutt Collection: **195**, photo courtesy the Seattle Art Museum

St. Louis Art Museum: **100**, Anonymous Gift

Ira Simon: **48 bottom and jacket back**, courtesy Historical Design, Inc., New York

Society of Colonial Wars in the State of New York: **74–75**

Sotheby's: **31 bottom, 40, 41, 48 top, 50, 57 bottom, 66, 83, 104, 126, 132 bottom, 137, 139, 142, 148 right, 150, 154, 163, 177 top, 179, 197, 216 bottom, 223 bottom**

Tiffany & Co. Archives: **2; 8–9; 17; 24–25; 29; 31 top; 32; 35 center and bottom; 36; 38; 44–45; 47; 53 left; 54–56 (56 top** photo Sotheby's**); 57 top; 59 bottom; 60 bottom; 61; 65 bottom; 69; 71; 72 bottom; 73; 80 bottom; 82–83 (83** photo Sotheby's**); 93; 95; 101; 106 top; 109–10; 113–14; 116; 119–21; 124 drawing; 126** (photo Sotheby's)**; 127; 129; 130 top; 132 top right; 134 right; 136; 137 drawing; 138; 140 top; 144 bottom; 145; 146–47; 164; 168; 170–71; 173; 174 drawing; 175** (photo Sotheby's)**; 176 drawing bottom; 181–82; 187 right** (photo Museum of Fine Arts, Boston) **and drawing top; 191–93 drawings; 196; 200** (photo Sotheby's)**; 205; 208 bottom; 210; 216 top; 219 right; 221; 223 top; 227–30; 234; 238; 243 top; 244–45; 248**, *Tiffany Bluebook* 1981; **253**, *Tiffany Bluebook* 1985; **257; 265**

Tiffany's *150 Years* by John Loring (Doubleday & Co., 1987): **1; 14; 78; 99; 148 left; 187 bottom left; 239**

Toledo Museum of Art, Toledo, Ohio: **37**, Decorative Arts Purchase Fund and Museum Art Fund (1985.32)

University of California, Berkeley, Hearst Mining Building: **16**

Westminster Kennel Club: **117 top**

White House Collection, courtesy White House Historical Association: **108**

Yale University Art Gallery: **39**, Mrs. Alfred E. Bissell, Mr. and Mrs. Samuel Schwartz, Mr. and Mrs. E. Martin Wunsch and the American Arts Purchase Funds

Photograph Credits

Noel Allum: **27, 35 top, 67, 72 top, 102, 133, 161, 166, 178**

AP / Wide World Photos: **259**

© James Biever / NFL Photos: **258**

Eric Boman: **author's photograph**

Adam Campanella: **2**

John Corbett: **7**

Billy Cunningham: **74–75, 88, 97 left, 98, 106 top, 149, 151, 152–3, 192 top, 218 bottom, 224, 229, 237, 249, 251**

Phil Garfield: **266**

William Geiger: **107**

Jesse Gerstein: **14, 78, 110 bottom, 148 left, 187 bottom left**

Ben Grishaaver, Leiden, The Netherlands: **96**

Robert Hashimoto: **124 bottom, 125**

Elizabeth Heyert: **1**

Hiro: **256**, © Kuma Enterprise

© Mark Humphries: **263 bottom**

Tom Jenkins: **46 bottom, 58, 211, 212 bottom**

David Kelley: **15, 68, 123 top, 188, 208, 223 top, 229**

Shecter Lee: **front jacket, 87, 90–91, 115, 165**

Leigh Photo and Imaging, LLC: **226 bottom**

Kevin Logan: **99, 105, 239**

Colin McCrae: **16, 30, 34, 42 bottom, 51**

Fernando Medina / NBA Photos: **261**

NBA Photos: **263 top**

© 2000 Newsday, Inc., Reprinted with Permission: **262 top**

Tony Quinn / SoccerPix USA © 2000: **262 bottom**

Douglas Rosa: **254**

Walter Thomson: **54, 117 top, 232**

Steve Vento, Vento Photography, Inc.: **216 top**

Tom Wachs © 1994: **6**

ACKNOWLEDGMENTS

The author and Tiffany & Co. would like to thank William R. Chaney, chairman of Tiffany's, and Michael Kowalski, president and chief executive officer of Tiffany's, for their confidence and support.

We must next give special recognition, in alphabetical order, to: Eric Erickson, whose invaluable aesthetic judgments did so much to single out truly masterful works from the almost countless legions of trophy, commemorative, exhibition, and presentation silver produced by Tiffany's shops over a one-hundred-fifty-year period, and for his relentless dedication to tracking down so many seemingly lost masterpieces; to Kay Freeman for her thorough, remarkable, and revealing research on the careers of each of Tiffany's great nineteenth-century silversmiths, which brings back to light the careers of these important and colorful figures in the history of the American decorative arts; and to Rollins Maxwell for his enlightened captions, which brilliantly illuminate so much of America's sporting, business, social, and artistic history. This is as much their book as it is the author's, and the history of silver in America will forever be richer in scope and texture for their praiseworthy efforts.

We are also grateful to Annamarie Sandecki, Tiffany's director of archives, for her help with the ongoing adventure of exploring Tiffany & Co.'s treasure trove of archival documents, drawings, and photographs; Louisa Bann, Tiffany's manager of research services, for her generous-spirited support and guidance in the bewildering complexities of our archives; Stephanie Carson, registrar of the archives, for orchestrating the reproduction of archival materials; MaryAnn Aurora for her perception and diplomacy in maintaining order in the chaotic array of materials and personalities that had to be united to create this book; Margaret Rennolds Chace, vice-president and managing editor of Harry N. Abrams, for her unflagging support of the concept of this book and of all involved with its realization; Elisa Urbanelli, our editor, for the clarity of her vision and for her sustained and unqualified enthusiasm during the book's development; Carol Ann Robson, our designer at Abrams, for her genius at discovering all the visual echoes and stylish details in the history of Tiffany silver and for articulating them with her own mixture of visual grace, charm, and panache, which give the book the magnificence announced by its title; and Sharon AvRutick, our copyeditor, for her prowess at maintaining simplicity, clarity, and continuity throughout inherently complex texts and captions.

The following were invaluable in providing illustrations and deserve our thanks: Christie's and Sotheby's for the use of their vast and unique photograph archives; Daniel Roschnotti of the New York Yacht Club, whose collections include so many of Tiffany's great trophies, for his much-needed help in illustrating this book; Dr. B. Woelderink, director of The Royal Collection, The Hague; The Art Institute of Chicago; the Kunstgewerbemuseum, Berlin; The Brooklyn Museum of Art; Anita Ellis of the Cincinnati Art Museum; The Dallas Museum of Art; the Museum of Fine Arts, Boston; the Museum of Fine Arts, Houston; The Philadelphia Museum of Art; The New Jersey State Museum; The Los Angeles County Museum of Art; Marguerite Lavin of the Museum of the City of New York; Jonathan Harding and The Century Association; Nota Biederman, Daniel S. Curtis, and N. David Sherrill of the Society of Colonial Wars in the State of New York; William F. Stifel of the Westminster Kennel Club; Scott C. Steward and Harvard's Porcellian Club; Gary Anderson and the Civilian Marksmanship Program; Nelson & Nelson, New York; Michael Weller of Argentum, San Francisco; Mrs. Sean J. Eagan; and D. Brenton Simons.

Considerable thanks also goes to the New York Public Library, America's quintessential archive, where so much of the information in this book was discovered by Kay Freeman and Rollins Maxwell; to Charles Carpenter, Jr. and Charles L. Venable, whose splendid and pioneering books *Tiffany Silver* and *Silver in America* (Abrams, 1994) so beautifully charted the territories further explored and detailed by our own book; to D. Albert Soeffing for sharing his panoramic knowledge of the history of American silver; to Katherine S. Howe, Michael K. Brown, and David B. Warren's work on American silver trophies, *Marks of Achievement* (Abrams, 1987), which was also of invaluable aid; and, last but not at all least, to Francis Safford and the department of American Decorative Arts at the Metropolitan Museum of Art for all their generosity in enabling us to illustrate the many masterpieces of Tiffany silver in the museum's permanent collection.